"As an agency owner, I have to concentrate on [the] day-to-day. Mike helped us focus on strategies that are profitable and give us a clear direction."

Steve Grice, President, Grice Financial Group, Charlotte, North Carolina

"Mike's presentations are dynamic and get our advisors thinking about a different approach to their practices."

Leo Carten, Vice President, Insurance Services, Piper Jaffray, Minneapolis, Minnesota

"Mike has helped us move our agency from a service organization to a marketing organization, which we desperately needed in order to grow. With his business planning system I now know exactly how I'll grow my agency 75% this year."

Bill Conwell, President, Conwell & Associates, Birmingham, Alabama

"[Mike] brings our producers dynamic business development ideas that can have dramatic results in their practices."

Tom Mayer, President, Direct Benefits, St. Paul, Minnesota

Ultimate Breakthrough Planning
The Business Funnel Approach

Mike Ferrell

SCARLETTA PRESS

Minneapolis
www.scarlettapress.com

Scarletta Press
10 South 5th Street, Suite 1105, Minneapolis, MN 55402 USA
Visit our website at www.scarlettapress.com

Library of Congress Cataloging-in-Publication Data

Ferrell, Mike.
  Ultimate breakthrough planning : the business funnel approach /
Mike Ferrell.
     p.   cm.
  Includes bibliographical references and index.
  ISBN 978-0-9798249-0-6
1. Business planning. 2. Strategic planning. I. Title.
  HD30.28.F475 2008
  658.4'012--dc22

                                                          2008022484

ISBN 13: 978-0-9798249-0-6
ISBN 10: 0-9798249-0-7

Book design by Chris Long for Mighty Media Inc., Minneapolis, MN
First edition
10 9 8 7 6 5 4 3 2 1
Manufactured in Canada

For Mom and Dad, and Susan—always by my side

Contents

Chapter 5

Chapter 6

Preface

Since reluctantly accepting the fact that I was not going to make my fortune as a professional golfer or, for that matter, a priest, I have been making a splendid living by presenting seminars and workshops on the subject of business growth. The success I've enjoyed since giving up those youthful dreams has taught me that objective planning and everyday action produce results every bit as satisfying as more romantic pursuits. Becoming a business consultant was the best thing I ever did! After much trial and error, and a great deal of troubleshooting with struggling businesses, I found myself focusing on six key elements— those found in this book—that are necessary for any company's survival and long-term profitability. In the course of building my presentations I developed a process that helps businesspeople focus objective energy on the things they need to do to create sustained growth. The process is simple enough, yet most business owners fail to develop anything like it without coaching.

For the past twenty-two years I have worked with many types of businesses, organizations and sales practices. During that time I've seen many successes and unfortunately, as many failures. What I try to provide for my clients—business owners, managers or anyone trying to grow a business—is a dynamic new method of thinking about business planning, one that throws out the old model of adhering blindly to a sometimes faulty business plan, and focuses on the six specific areas that will help grow their businesses. I introduce the notion of a "funnel approach" that takes the guesswork out of daily execution. As you read through the chapters, gaining full understanding of *The Business Funnel Approach*, you'll appreciate how relatively simple and amazingly useful it will be in improving your own endeavors.

The idea behind this book has been years in the making. Probably as far back as 1986, when I started my first company, I suspected that there would be a book in my future. I know so much more now than I did then, but when I finally started writing I received a shock. I thought that pulling my seminar presentations together into book form would be fairly simple. Boy, was I naive—writing a book like this is tough, even with the help of kind and sympathetic editors. However, after much toil, I culled what I hope is the most useful material from years of presentations customized to a wide variety of clients who all shared the same goal: the development of sustainable business growth.

I have always done extensive research in pursuit of methods and processes that might help my clients take their businesses to higher levels. I have also had the opportunity to use *The Business Funnel Approach* in several different start-ups, and what I have found—and this certainly is not rocket science—is that owners persist in starting businesses which they fundamentally have very little idea how they are going to grow. They all followed the same route of creating a business plan designed to make their bankers and investors happy, but in reality that type of business plan seldom helps with the actual meat and potatoes of everyday growth. As I examined the failures of companies with seemingly sound business plans I found that there really was no articulated formula or systematic approach to honest, feet-on-the-ground *action*. Who will write weekly plans? Who will bring in interns? Who will write press releases? Who will lick the stamps and stick them on the envelopes? Most businesses start up with an attitude of "Build it and they will come." That's fine if you live in a field of dreams and believe in friendly ghosts, but healthy business growth must rely on more than faith, hope and charity.

Sure, there are plenty of good manuals available, written by experts and dedicated to marketing, sales, finance, service, pricing, management and every other facet of business. However, I found no useful advice among the mountain of business books I studied that suggested bringing together the key elements that are required for business success. I found nothing tangible about shaping those elements into an executable process that gives the person starting or running a business better than a snowball's chance in hell of success.

There are plenty of business success stories, but for every success there are four failures. I have found that in most cases when a business or sales practice fails, it is because management either had no idea where it was going in the first place, or knew exactly where to go but failed to execute the strategies necessary to get there.

So this book is about nothing more than execution!

Put simply, it is about creating a game plan and executing that game plan to perfection. Although this is easily said, it is not so easily done; hard work is required. And yes, *The Business Funnel Approach* outlined in this book is relatively simple, but in order to execute it to perfection you must work on your business every single day. Please note that I said work *on* your business not work *in* your business. The difference is immediately apparent as soon as the distinction is pointed out. Every single day you must do what needs to be done to execute your plan, while always remaining cognizant of the plan itself and how it will impact your business. I have seen the process work extremely well on many occasions, but I have also seen it fail because the person or persons executing the plan lose focus on what they need to be doing and, excuse the cliché, just plain drop the ball. No plan works well when the human element fails. But if you use *The Business Funnel Approach* to create the focus you need on the things you need to focus on, and then do the specific things that need to happen each and every day, you will see your business thrive. Keep focused and execute the plan, and I wish you success.

The Business Funnel Approach

The Traditional Approach Is Flawed

In 2005, 544,800 small businesses closed for a variety of reasons: lack of capital, lack of customers, poor location, bad service, or the wrong product. How many of these small businesses could have avoided this fate if they'd had an easy-to-follow plan, or blueprint, that would have helped them succeed? There have been hundreds—if not thousands—of business books written about running businesses, and there are nearly as many software models and programs a small business can use to create a business plan—not to mention all the business gurus and consul-

---

THE REASON FOR SO MUCH BUSINESS FAILURE IS ONE SIMPLE THING: LACK OF EXECUTION.

---

tants available. That being the case, why is there so much failure?

After twenty-two years of working on, working in, owning, and observing businesses, I believe the reason for so much business failure is one simple thing: lack of execution. The old axiom "most businesses don't plan to fail, they fail to plan" isn't completely true. Certainly many businesses *don't* plan and therefore never truly know where they are headed; but many businesses *do* put together a detailed business plan and still fail. The problem is not in the plan, it is in the execution of the plan. The businesses that fail focus solely on the goals and results they want to achieve and forget about the activity that needs to be done to achieve the goals. Had they incorporated the execution components into the plan and then passionately implemented those components, not only would they still be around, they would be thriving.

An Approach For Bankers and Investors

Many businesses go through the business planning process when they first begin, or when they are looking for capital and investors. Unfortunately the standard model creates a business plan suitable for impressing bankers and investors, but it will not really help the business owner create and grow a successful business. The typical plan is designed to focus on executive summaries, marketing plans, sales projections, and cash flow models. Rarely does it address the business owner's vision of what he or she wants to create, let alone executable steps that will help him or her achieve that vision.

Lack of Action
in the Traditional Approach

Through discipline, successful companies create processes and systems they can repeat over and over again. I remember playing in a Pro-Am golf tournament several years ago and hitting practice balls on the range next to Gary Player. I watched him hit shot after shot to the exact same place and distance and finally I asked him why he was doing that. His response was that when he competes he wants to be able to focus on the conditions and managing the course and his emotions, without having to think about the mechanics of his swing; therefore, he disciplined his swing by practicing the mechanics over and over again so that it became automatic. This type of discipline is vital to creating and building a successful business.

In Jim Collins' book *Good to Great*, one of the concepts the author examines in great companies is the "culture of discipline." Collins says:

> ... all companies have a culture, some companies have discipline, but few companies have a culture of discipline. When you have disciplined people, you don't need hierarchy. When you have disciplined thought, you don't need bureaucracy. When you have disciplined action, you don't

need excessive controls. When you combine a culture of discipline with an ethic of entrepreneurship, you get the magical alchemy of great performance. (13)

In other words, he's talking about *execution*. What I mean by *execution* in this book is the performance of indicated tasks according to encoded instructions. This definition is what I mean when I discuss "executing a business plan." The problem is that most business plans don't have specific instructions, and this is where they fail; they take a 30,000-foot view of the business but never get down to the details or specific tasks that need to be done to get that business to look like what they've drawn up on paper. Bill Walsh, the former coach of the San Francisco 49ers, is credited in building a dynasty, but he also was one of the first coaches to actually script out the first twenty plays his team would run in a game. He didn't care what the other team did; he was going to execute his game plan. A successful business plan should do the same thing in scripting out the specific things that need to happen for that business to be successful. That is executing a business plan.

Ultimate Breakthrough Planning
Creates Action

As a former golf professional I believe business planning is like being a good golfer. Good golfers don't just show up on the first tee and say the goal is to break par; they understand that a number of things must go into their preparation before they can ever break par: learning and honing their swing, understanding course management and controlling their thoughts and emotions. They do not focus on the end result; they focus on the specific tasks required to achieve the end result.

In my experience working with many types of businesses, I have found that the successful ones typically have two things going for them: they have an objective and determined focus, and they have everyday discipline that helps them stick to what they are trying to accomplish. They have a vision and game plan they follow religiously, and they have planned exactly where they are headed.

In the early 1990s, I had the opportunity to work with Adams Golf before their name got really big. Barney Adams, the president and founder of the company, was relentless in his focus on technology as a clear point of differentiation in club design. He was talking about things like "moment of inertia" long before other manufacturers were emphasizing this in their club designs. By sticking to that focus and staying ahead of the industry, he was able to build a successful company and brand.

The Business Funnel Approach, which seeks to define this script or blueprint for a variety of business types, looks at Six Key Elements of business success. These Six Key Elements will be addressed throughout this book, and they are summarized in the following pages.

Six Key Elements

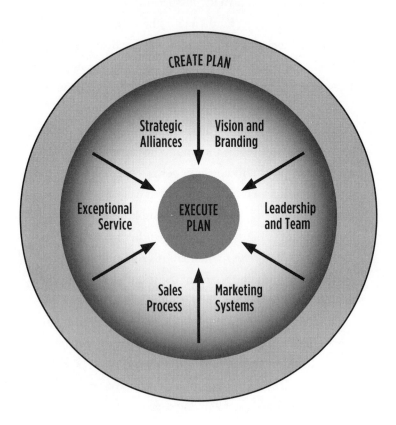

Vision and Branding

Vision and branding are the first, critical steps in determining what your business will look like, what you want it to do and how you want it to function. Your vision statement defines what you are trying to accomplish and communicates that vision to your team. Your brand states who you are, what you do, how you do it and how your business is different from your competitors. This message is communicated to your customers and prospects. By creating a brand you begin the process of differentiating your business. If you don't have a clear vision and brand, your business will constantly be taken on a winding road that leads to frustration.

Leadership and Team

The most critical element in any business is its personnel; people drive the company forward. Your leadership, management and vision will be incorporated into concepts that will help you clearly communicate with your team to make them more effective. By also understanding your strengths and your team's strengths, you can manage your business in a way that maximizes everyone's strengths, rather than minimizes their weaknesses. Without clear leadership and an effective team, you will be constantly putting out fires with personnel and struggling to get the right people on board and in the right seats.

Marketing Systems

Marketing systems are the keys to letting the world know who you are and what you have to offer. By creating systems that ensure your marketing is done consistently across a variety of mediums, you give yourself a much better chance at succeeding. Your marketing systems are essential to not only drive new business but to also expand on current customer relationships and gain new insights into markets and opportunities. One of the most important elements of any business is marketing. If you don't have a specific plan on how you will effectively market your business you will constantly experience peaks and valleys.

Sales Process

By understanding why your customers buy, and how they buy, you can effectively create a sales process that will lead to increased business and also stronger relationships with your customers. You will also make your salespeople more effective and give them a better chance to succeed. You can build a sales process no matter what type of business you are running. Whether you are selling face-to-face or there is little customer interaction, such as in online sales, the easier it is for people to do business with you the better your chances of success. Without a sales process you will constantly be fighting to achieve your sales goals and will not understand why you're having problems.

Exceptional Service

Service is the proverbial double-edged sword—if you don't deliver good service, your business is in trouble. Delivering exceptional service means taking good service to a higher level. The first step to exceptional service is defining what exceptional service means in your business, and then communicating that to your team. Getting your team involved in this part of the plan is essential; without them you can't deliver exceptional service. Exceptional service creates raving fans and raving fans create more business. If you don't deliver exceptional service you will constantly be looking for new customers.

Strategic Alliances

Determining what you do well—and what you don't—is the first step to creating strategic alliances. Strategic alliances are relationships with people and businesses that can do things better than you can do, which frees you up to follow your strengths. Strategic alliances may also be partnerships that create new markets, goods or services that you can offer your customers. Strategic alliances really help you take your business to the highest level by leveraging the expertise, services, products and markets of another party.

Now that we've defined the Six Key Elements, let's learn how to apply them to the Business Funnel Approach.

Take the Ultimate Breakthrough Planning Business Analysis at
www.ultimatebreakthroughplanning.com

The Business Funnel Approach Defined

The Business Funnel Approach provides a step-by-step means to correlate the successful execution of the Six Key Elements. Since every organization is unique, individual businesses must formulate specific processes for putting these six elements into action. A manager or business owner reading this segment should immediately know what is being referred to and will probably be jotting down notes beside these diagrams to incorporate later into the organization's business plan. Below is the "big picture" model of the Business Planning Funnel, but bear in mind that it's useful to visualize each of the Six Key Elements, mentioned earlier, with its own Business Planning Funnel.

Identify Priorities
Set Goals and Objectives
Define Your Strategies
Determine Your Tools
Communicate and Train
Create Tasks and Timelines
Keep Score and Communicate Results
Reward Success

The Business Planning Funnel gives the business plan a very different look, first by laying out a specific process for building the plan, and then showing how to execute the plan successfully. This graphic approach gives business owners something they can look at and use every day as a working tool. The funnel is designed to walk them through each step so nothing is overlooked concerning what needs to be done, how it will be done, who will do it, what support will be provided, what the expected results are, and how those results will be tracked and rewarded when achieved. This approach focuses on the exact actions that need to be executed in order for the plan and the business to succeed.

When a football coach designs a game plan he doesn't focus on the eventual outcome of the game; he focuses on the specific offensive, defensive and special teams plays that need to happen to affect the eventual outcome in his favor. Too many business owners focus their plan on the eventual outcome and skip the specific steps needed to achieve those results. Each month they look at their results and cannot figure out why they are not hitting their numbers. The reason is they have no plan for execution. In the words of author Robert Ringer, "nothing happens until something moves" (the subtitle to his book *Action!*).

THE BUSINESS PLANNING FUNNEL GIVES THE
BUSINESS PLAN A VERY DIFFERENT LOOK,
FIRST BY LAYING OUT A SPECIFIC PROCESS FOR
BUILDING THE PLAN, AND THEN SHOWING HOW
TO EXECUTE THE PLAN SUCCESSFULLY.

The funnel sets down each specific action necessary to arrive at the goal. Whether you are trying to implement better marketing, improve customer service or strengthen the role of the leader/manager, the funnel can be used the same way. Let's examine the process for creating funnels:

Identify Priorities

How do you define your priorities? The first question you should ask is, "What are the most critical things I need to do to grow my business?" Your priorities should reflect the most critical issues that need to be resolved over the next six months. You should focus on no more than four priorities. More than that and you'll be spread too thinly.

Some questions to consider when determining your priorities are:

- Should I focus internally or externally?
- Is it more important to focus on strengthening my team or attracting new business?
- Where is my business in the business cycle?

The answer to this last question may affect whether you should focus on growth, maintaining market share, pursuing new markets, or succession issues.

Every six months, reevaluate your priorities using these questions again. Your plan may always have some of the same priorities, such as marketing systems and service, whereas training may only be an issue as new employees are brought in or new systems and processes are incorporated.

Set Goals and Objectives

In setting goals you are defining your final destination. Your plan will focus on how you are going to arrive at that destination. The first thing you need to determine is the measurements you are going to use: revenue, sales, profits, etc. Your goals should reflect your business. I have always suggested to my clients that the easiest way to determine the best measurement is to identify what pays the bills and what goes in your pocket. These have always been the best yardsticks.

In goal setting you must challenge yourself. In my workshops I always say that if you set a goal to grow 10, 15, or 20%, you are really just challenging yourself to work a little harder, but when you set a goal of growing your business 50 or 100% you are challenging yourself to change the way you do business.

In Brian Tracy's book *Goals*, he says the most important thing to remember is to avoid the "comfort zone ... by setting big, challenging goals" (114). Until you move out of your comfort zone you will never truly take your business to its highest level, and the only way to reach that level is to rethink the way you do business.

In the book *The Power of Focus*, authors Jack Canfield, Mark Victor Hansen and Les Hewitt say:

> *A goal is an ongoing pursuit of a worthy objective until accomplished. Consider the individual words that make up this sentence. "Ongoing" means a process, because goals take time. "Pursuit" indicates a chase may be involved.*

There will likely be some obstacles and hurdles to over-come. "Worthy" shows that the chase will be worthwhile, that there's enough reward at the end to endure the tough times. "Until accomplished" suggests you'll do whatever it takes to get the job done. Not always easy, but essential if you want a life full of outstanding accomplishments. (61)

Setting objectives becomes a question of what you want to accomplish. You need to consider what you want your business to look like, what you would like to change about your business, and what specific objectives can help you achieve these goals. These objectives could be new markets, new products, better service, or anything you think could help you achieve your goals. The reason objectives are so important is they allow you to start focusing on the Six Key Elements and choosing which of those elements is going to be the focus of your plan.

Define Your Strategies

What is strategy? It is the method you will use to grow your business. When we look at strategy we can focus on each of the Six Key Elements and define methods that might be employed in each of these areas. For instance, in marketing systems, a strategy may be the way you open up a key new market, maybe it will be a new sales approach, maybe it will be a new product or maybe it will be a new concept. This piece of The Business Planning Funnel is absolutely critical because your strategy will dictate everything that follows: all your actions will be determined by the strategies you choose. Your strategies should be clearly directed by your chosen objectives, and each of those objectives should spawn strategies. If your objective is to improve customer service, then a strategy may be to improve employee training, or the implementation of new customer interface systems. Another way to think about strategy is to consider the things you are currently doing and what you are trying to achieve. For example, what are you trying to accomplish by the various forms of marketing you are using? Is your goal new customers, more market share, better customer relations? Again, the strategies flow down from your priorities, your goals and your objectives.

When deciding how many strategies you should employ, think about what you and your team can realistically do. Do not have so many strategies that you lose focus. The more time and resources you and your team can devote to a few strategies, the more successful you will be. Many business owners make the mistake of trying to do everything all at once, but eventually they will lose the battle because it is impossible to focus on everything.

Determine Tools

Once you have determined what strategies you are going to focus on, then it is time to get down to the nuts and bolts of how you are going to implement them. The tools you will use are the specific overall tactics that will advance each of your chosen strategies. If your strategy is to improve customer service by shorter turnaround time, the tools you use to accomplish that may be a specific employee-training program, or a new process that will fulfill orders faster. These are specific tools you will use to move through the funnel.

Your tools should be concrete activities that will be clearly defined by action. However, the tools are not to be confused with more in-depth actions, which we will cover in a following section. The tools are the things you and your team will use consistently in the day-to-day operation of your business.

Communicate and Train

This is one of the key steps most businesses miss! Once they put into play the tools they have decided to use, they have a tendency to jump right in and assume the rest of the team will come along for the ride. Communicating with and training your team is critical because if they don't know what you are trying to do, why should they cooperate? At this point in your funnel you should have a pretty clear vision of what you are trying to accomplish, and communicating that message to your team is essential. You can communicate individually or as a group, but getting a buy-in from your team is critical. Your team needs to know first, how and why things are going to happen, and second, when they will happen and who will be responsible.

At this point training is key. It's important to make sure the people who are responsible for carrying out the actions are capable of carrying them out. We will touch more on team training when we examine the key element of leadership and team. Suffice it to say that if you don't have your team on board with you, it will be very difficult to succeed.

Create Tasks and Timelines

We are now down to the nitty-gritty. Tasks and timelines are the specific things that need to be done to carry out each of the tools. The easiest way to explain this is by using an example. Let's say that one of your tools is a direct mail campaign. Your tasks and timelines will be the things that need to happen to carry out that campaign:

- Create the mailing list
- Develop the letters
- Address the letters
- Stamp the letters
- Mail the letters

In tasks and timelines you must be as specific as possible. Each of the tasks needs to be assigned to a person with a specific timeline for accomplishing it. In order for any of your tools to work the way they are supposed to, the tasks and timelines need to be developed, communicated and executed.

Keep Score and Communicate Results

Your funnel is now operating and your team is moving forward. It is time to start keeping score, but first you need to understand the manner in which you will keep score. The most critical element of making your plan successful is measuring the right things. Earlier I said that you need to focus on activities, not results; here is where that comes into play. In order to keep score of the right things, you need to determine some key milestones for your activities, such as number of mailings, number of new customers, turnaround time, number of sales, number of hits on your website. These are the types of things you need to measure because they tie directly to your strategies and your objectives. Experience tells us that if you hit the milestones you set within each of the strategies you are focusing on, you will almost always make or exceed your goals. In 2001 my partner and I adopted this process in our brokerage agency, and by focusing on the actions, not the goals, we were able to grow our business 167%. We have continued to grow it exponentially in each subsequent year.

Once you have your scorekeeping down, the other key component is to communicate the results. It always amazes me that when I ask my clients' employees how they think the business is doing, most of them, even the key ones, are frequently in the dark. If you do not tell your people how the company is faring, it is very difficult for them to remain invested and stay focused. Most of the time employees want to be able to go above and beyond to help the business grow, especially if they are being rewarded.

> Find more tools and resources at www.ultimatebreakthroughplanning.com

Reward Success

The last aspect of your funnel is rewarding success. If you want to grow your business through the process of building, executing and keeping score, then the last aspect—rewarding success—becomes the icing on the cake. In order to get real commitment from your employees you must show them you care about them. Zig Ziglar, one of the great motivational speakers in the business world, said in a 1987 speech, "if you help enough people get what they want, you will get what you want." You don't have to give away the farm, but a reward system that encourages your team to not only execute the plan but to do it with passion and a desire to succeed, is the key to true success.

IMPORTANT REMINDER:
Keep the Plan Flexible

The last thing to remember when creating your funnel is to keep your plan flexible. Most business plans look like they were created in a vacuum where nothing changes and adjustments are never made. Of course any business owner knows that's true for about the first five minutes, but what happens when all hell breaks loose? Your plan should be reevaluated every six months, which allows you time to

---

FOCUSING ON THE SIX KEY ELEMENTS AND ORGANIZING THEM INTO A BUSINESS PLANNING FUNNEL TAKES YOU FROM YOUR ORIGINAL PLAN TO YOUR GOALS.

---

implement and execute the plan but also gives you the opportunity to assess, adjust and refocus your plan twice a year. You can do it less often, but if you do I suggest you limit the number of priorities and strategies on which you focus.

Focusing on the Six Key Elements and organizing them using the Business Funnel Approach takes you from your original plan to your goals.

Following is an outline of the materials we will be discussing. In this book each of the Six Key Elements has its own chapter, and each chapter ends with an explanation of how to apply the Business Funnel Approach to the element in question. This outline is designed to emphasize both the order in which the Six Key Elements should be addressed and the order to be followed in resolving the components of each.

First Key Element: Vision and Branding

- The Challenge: The Funnel at Work

- Where Do You Want to Go?

- Create a Vision Statement

- Communicate Your Vision

- Branding: Where the Rubber Hits the Road

- Create Your Branding Message

- Now What? Communicating Your Brand

- Putting it All in a Funnel

- The Answer: The Funnel in Action

Second Key Element: Leadership and Team

- The Challenge: The Funnel at Work
- What Is Leadership? Why Is it Important in Your Plan?
- *StrengthsFinder*
- Build Your Team and Play to Their Strengths
- Communicate Your Plan and Get Buy-In
- Putting it All in a Funnel
- The Answer: The Funnel in Action

Third Key Element: Marketing Systems

- The Challenge: The Funnel at Work
- Why Market?
- Analyze Where You Are: Identify Priorities
- Create a Marketing Process: Set Goals and Objectives
- Define Strategies
- Determine Tools
- Communicate and Train
- Create Tasks and Timelines
- Keep Score and Communicate Results
- Reward Success
- Putting it All in a Funnel
- The Answer: The Funnel in Action

Fourth Key Element: Sales Process

- The Challenge: The Funnel at Work
- What Exactly is a Sales Process?
- Marketing Gets Them in the Door, Sales Makes Them Customers
- Identify Priorities
- Understanding Your Process
- Set Goals and Objectives
- Customers: Your Greatest Asset
- Define Strategies
- Try Diverse Processes
- Determine Tools
- Communicate and Train
- Create Tasks and Timelines
- Keep Score and Communicate Results
- Reward Success
- The Answer: The Funnel in Action

Fifth Key Element: Exceptional Service

- The Challenge: The Funnel at Work
- What is Exceptional Service?
- Service and Vision
- Identify Priorities
- Perception Turns into Reality

- Set Goals and Objectives
- Define Strategies
- Create Client Experiences
- Determine Tools
- Communicate and Train
- Create Tasks and Timelines
- Keep Score and Communicate Results
- Reward Success
- The Answer: The Funnel in Action

Sixth Key Element: Strategic Alliances

- The Challenge: The Funnel at Work
- What Am I Doing That Someone Else Could Do More Effectively?
- What Strategic Alliances Can I Form to Grow My Business?
- Identify Priorities
- Set Goals and Objectives
- Define Strategies
- Determine Tools
- Communicate and Train
- Create Tasks and Timelines
- Keep Score and Communicate Results
- Reward Success
- The Answer: The Funnel in Action

Most Important: Execution

It should be clear by now that the *Business Funnel Approach* IS ALL ABOUT ACTION. Execution of your plan is essential to the success of this funneling process. However, if you try to accomplish everything at once, and all by yourself, you will become overwhelmed, the distinctions so carefully laid out will blur together and you will risk chaos. Consider the following:

- Focus on a different strategy each month
- Promote company workshops
- Create marketing and sales blueprints
- Keep score
- Focus on the activities that generate results

Key Milestones

- What's a milestone?
- How do you create them?
- Communicating the results
- What do you do if success is eluding you?
- The six-month plan

For a sample of the Business Planning Funnel go to
www.ultimatebreakthroughplanning.com

SUMMARY:
THE BUSINESS FUNNEL APPROACH

- Business planning should be focused on the activities needed to achieve the goals and objectives that are set.

- The business plan should be as detailed as possible regarding activity.

- The business plan must be flexible enough to be changed when necessary.

- The plan should be reevaluated every six months to allow focus in different areas.

- Focus on action: the results will follow.

1

First Key Element:
Vision and Branding

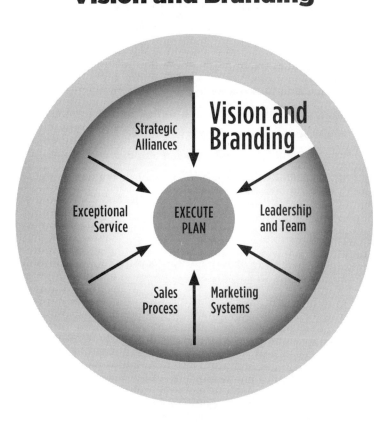

The Challenge: The Funnel at Work

I had an opportunity to work with a client whose company sold wholesale life insurance products to agents and financial advisors. The business had been started by the owner's father, who built it up by offering good service and competitive term insurance. When my client took over, term insurance was becoming a commodity product sold almost exclusively on price. In addition, profit margins were shrinking on this product line. He understood that he had to become more of a provider of insurance solutions, encompassing a full range of insurance products including term, universal, whole life, disability and long term care. When we began working together, he had recently hired a new external salesperson, a young, energetic woman, who, despite coming across as highly competent, was nevertheless quite green when it came to insurance brokerage. My client's challenge was to establish a revised vision and brand for his business—to create a story that would redefine the company for him, his new salesperson and their clients.

I coached my client to start by focusing on the following questions:

- Why did you start this particular business?

- What did you want to accomplish when you started this business?
  - Did you want personal freedom?
  - Did you want to dominate a market?
  - Did you have a better product?

- Did you want to offer your employees a better place to work?
- Did you want to build something for your children?
- Did you want to do something good for society?

The answers to questions like these will help determine your business goals. Once you have answered them, the next step is to create a statement that clarifies and supports your answers.

Where Do You Want to Go?

A few years ago Microsoft ran an ad campaign, asking, "Where do you want to go?" That question should be the starting point for any business planning process. If you don't know where you want to go, how are you going to get there? As Yogi Berra once said, "If you don't know where you're going, you'll wind up somewhere else." Unfortunately many business owners wind up somewhere else because they have not decided what they want their business to look like.

Create a Vision Statement

Composing a short but well articulated "vision statement" is the process of clearly mapping out, and then refining what you want your business to look like—what its values and mission will be. By answering the above questions, you will be able to develop a statement that allows you to keep in mind what you are trying to accomplish, as well as create a guide for your partners and employees to follow.

Your vision statement is not just a laundry list of what you manufacture and sell, or even how you're going to do it. When I work with my clients on this process I want them to think about why they started the business in the first place; what do they ultimately want out of the business; what is their primary purpose for being in business? The vision statement becomes the basis for everything we do in creating a successful plan. It is the foundation that helps us envision all the other key elements and what they should look like, because they must reflect our core vision of what this business is.

Answering the questions listed above begins the process of creating your vision statement. Try to use simple, evocative language that communicates clearly. Remember also that your vision statement should reflect your customers. What does your business provide for your customers, and how does it do so? This vision statement should be a simple paragraph or two about your purpose, why you do what you do and how will it better your life, your employees' lives, your customers' lives and your community.

A vision statement is often called a mission statement, but a vision statement is more succinct than a mission statement. A vision statement should state specifically what the owner is trying to accomplish. Here is the vision statement that I helped the insurance broker create:

Our vision is to be the insurance brokerage leader in our region. We will do this by establishing strong relationships with our producers and delivering value to their practices. We will empower our employees to deliver that value to our producers, and we will promote goodwill in our community by giving back to it 5% of our earnings each year.

In this example we set the bar to be the leader in a particular region. Some vision statements are geared more toward numbers, such as this one I did for a manufacturing company:

Our vision is to grow our business to $10 million in revenue over the next five years. We will do this by delivering quality products to our customers, helping our employees grow to their potential and maintaining profitable yet competitive pricing in our products.

Vision statements come from the business owners; what they want to accomplish with their businesses, and what their visions were when they first started their companies.

COMMUNICATING YOUR VISION AND GETTING BUY-IN FROM YOUR TEAM IS EXTREMELY IMPORTANT. IF THIS HAS NOT BEEN DONE, IT NEEDS TO BE IDENTIFIED AS A PRIORITY IN YOUR BUSINESS PLAN.

Communicate Your Vision

Once you have created the vision statement, the next step is to communicate that vision to your partners and employees, which I'll hereafter refer to as your *team*. Make sure your team understands that your business has a purpose beyond simply putting money in your or their pockets. Everything you and your team do going forward is built around that purpose. In Ken Blanchard's book, *Leading at a Higher Level*, he talks about communicating your vision:

> *"In some organizations a vision statement may be found framed on the wall, but it provides no guidance, or worse, has nothing to do with the reality of how things really are. This turns people off. Visioning is an ongoing process; you need to keep talking about the vision and referring to it as much as possible." (30)*

A useful exercise to help your team understand the vision and purpose is to give team members copies of the vision statement and ask them to look at it for a few days and come up with one idea, based on their understanding of the vision, that could better position the business.

I worked with an insurance brokerage company and the owner said his vision was to establish an organization that was completely dedicated to growing his clients' business. He then approached his team, communicated his statement to them and asked them to come up with better ways to attain the company goal. One employee came back and said that if their sole purpose is to help their clients grow their businesses, why does 80% of their communication occur with the vendors and not the clients? She made a great point, and from there we went to work changing the way the company communicated with its clients.

Communicating your vision and getting buy-in from your team is extremely important. If this has not been done, it needs to be identified as a priority in your business plan.

Branding:
Where the Rubber Hits the Road

Branding is a popular topic these days on the business front. Everywhere you turn businesspeople are talking about branding. But what is branding? For large companies it is brand recognition; but for our purposes it represents, to use a wonderfully appropriate idiom, where the rubber hits the road.

Branding and your branding message should focus on who you are, what you do, how you do it, and what makes your company unique. By creating a branding message that is clearly communicated to your team and your custom-

---

BRANDING IS NOT ABOUT LOGOS OR PACKAGING; IT IS MUCH DEEPER. BRANDING IS ABOUT WHAT YOUR CUSTOMERS SHOULD FEEL.

---

ers, you begin the process of differentiation. Jerry Garcia of the rock group The Grateful Dead once said, "You don't want to be the best of the best, you want to be the only one that does what you do." Branding is about why you get up in the morning and why you go to work. It should reflect your passion for what you are doing.

Your branding message should clearly communicate why someone should do business with you. Branding is not about logos or packaging; it is much deeper. Branding is about what your customers should feel. It is about what makes you stand out when your competitors all look the same. In his book *Re-Imagine!*, Tom Peters says:

> *Branding is about nothing more (and nothing less) than heart. It's about passion, what you care about. It's about what's inside you and what's inside your company. (156)*

In order to create your branding message, you need to put yourself in your customers' shoes. What are they looking for, and how can you truly stand out in the crowd so they will see you? Branding is different from your vision statement: it is what your business does and how it differs from the competition.

Create Your Branding Message

The first step in creating your branding message is to go through a process that helps you truly determine what makes your business unique and identify potential points of differentiation between you and your competitors. Your branding message will have two distinct parts:

1. Who you are and what you do. This elevator speech will be the basis for your message.

2. Your full branding message, which will describe your credibility, resources and how you do what you do.

The following questions, each of which will be expanded upon in the following pages, will guide you in developing your branding message:

QUESTIONS TO ASK YOURSELF

- Who Are You?
- What Do You Do?
- How Are You Unique?
- How Do You Do What You Do?
- What Is Your Credibility?

Who Are You?

You must answer this question in two succinct sentences, riveting the essence of your business into the minds of yourself and potential customers. While recently working with a new client, we started with the fact that they were a community bank. As we examined the obvious a bit further, we realized they were also a full-service financial provider that went far beyond what is generally thought of as traditional community banking. Once we noticed what clearly defined them, a detail that had eluded everyone, the bank was able to re-brand and assure customers that they provided many more services than just traditional banking products.

As you think about who you are, put yourself in your customers' shoes and make sure that the message speaks to them and their needs.

What Do You Do?

Focus on the specific things you do from the perspective of your customers. Think conceptually about what it is you do. In my work with financial advisors I often ask them to think about how their clients perceive what they do. They don't just sell investments or manage money. They help their clients protect, grow and transfer their wealth.

Whatever succinct statement emerges from your thinking should say less about what your products are, and more about what the products do. If you sell widgets, say you sell widgets, but then focus on what those widgets do for your customers. The sooner your branding message moves away from price, product and performance and starts talking about value, solutions and exceptional service—and then is backed up with execution—the sooner your brand will be established.

Once you finish answering who you are and what

you do, prepare an "elevator speech," which summarizes these two sections in no more than three or four sentences. Imagine standing in an elevator when someone asks you what you do. In that brief ride you should be able to give them a concise and memorable response. Many times in my workshops people say, "But it sounds canned!" The key to having it not sound canned is repetition: the more you use it, the more familiar it becomes, enabling you to deliver it in a matter-of-fact manner that sounds comfortable and conversational.

Here is a sample of an elevator speech, which I helped a client create: *We work with financial professionals to help them help their clients protect, grow and transfer their wealth.* It is a simple statement that clearly shows what the company does; it condenses and fixes the company endeavor in the minds of both listener and speaker. The elevator speech I created for my own company is this: *I work with businesses to help them create focus in their strategic planning and business development, and I concentrate on six key areas and a unique planning process to help them achieve that focus.* The rest of the branding message then goes into the six areas and how I work in each of them.

THE SOONER YOUR BRANDING MESSAGE MOVES AWAY FROM PRICE, PRODUCT AND PERFORMANCE AND STARTS TALKING ABOUT VALUE, SOLUTIONS AND EXCEPTIONAL SERVICE—AND THEN IS BACKED UP WITH EXECUTION—THE SOONER YOUR BRAND WILL BE ESTABLISHED.

How Are You Unique?

Depending on your business, this is probably the hardest question to answer. However, the faster you answer it and put it into your message the closer you are to creating your brand. When thinking through this question consider the specific things you do and how you differ from your competitors. If you discover, after rigorously honest analysis, that you are not as unique as you need to be, find a way to be so and revise your business vision and message.

How Do You Do What You Do?

Once you have determined your uniqueness, combine that concept with how you do what you do. In this section of your branding message, focus on four or five bullet points. Once again put yourself in your customers' shoes and think about how they perceive what you do.

In my work with banks I encourage them to think about how the products and services they offer are beneficial to customers, such as providing capital to grow businesses or buy homes, or cash management tools such as checking and savings accounts.

The more you can offer in a unique and memorable way, the more it will mean to your customers, which will establish your brand in their eyes.

What Is Your Credibility?

How have you established your business? If you are new, what is your background and experience? It is vital in establishing your branding message that you discuss your credibility. Stress your expertise, your experience, your team's experience, your resources and alliances. This is where you tie your message together. It is also a great place to tie in a tag line—which, by the way, is not a branding message. You could say something like, "Our team has x years of experience and we have strategic partners that help us deliver our products and services," and then end with your tag line.

A tag line is a very simple statement that is created for people to remember and associate with you, your product or your company. Some examples of tag lines are: "Coke— It's the real thing," "Avis—We're number two. We try harder," and the tag line for my own company, "The Pinecrest Group—Creating Focus." You want your tag line to be a short, simple statement that is memorable.

Now What? Communicating Your Brand

The only way you create a brand in your business is to live it! Communicating your branding message to your team, your vendors, your customers and your prospects over and over again will establish your brand. But you must also embrace it. Everything you do in your business must follow your branding message. Display your branding message everywhere—on your walls, on your website, at trade shows, on your marketing materials—and have your team use it repeatedly until it becomes part of them.

Putting it All in a Funnel

Now we've talked about the importance of creating your vision statement and branding message. So how do you put it into the plan? The key to your breakthrough is the Business Funnel Approach.

Let's walk through what your vision and branding funnel might look like. In identifying priorities, creating your vision statement and branding message is the highest priority. And in doing this, you identify priorities within the areas of vision and branding. Once they are created, you then follow through by communicating them.

Your goals and objectives should include getting the message down and communicating and using it. As you move through the Business Funnel Approach, record your ideas at each step. Remember, this is a tool to help you create an execution plan.

When you define your strategies, think about the types of strategies you can use to create your vision statement and branding message. You should create your vision statement and communicate it to your team. By contrast, when creating your branding message, you should get as much input as possible from your team. Strategies might include brainstorming sessions, one-on-one meetings and all-employee meetings.

When assigning tasks and timelines, think about the creation of your message, how you're going to get your message out, what it will take to do that, and on what kind of timeline you're operating. Be realistic about the time this process will take.

Take each step of the Business Funnel Approach, put together your ideas and put them into a flow chart or spreadsheet that can be communicated to your team. You'll get better buy-in—which is critical for your branding. The earlier you get this material to your team, the better.

Once you've created your funnel for vision and branding, review it with your key team members, delegate the tasks and timelines, and outline the rewards and how you'll get participation from everyone.

Vision and branding is the first element in your overall plan; it is also one of the most crucial elements of your business because you don't want to "wind up somewhere else."

The Answer: The Funnel in Action

Now back to my term life insurance client: When I first asked him why he sold only that one product, he said that was what the company had always done. Therefore, we identified the primary priority: to create a message that would reposition his business as a problem solver, not a product supplier. Thus, our principal strategy was to create a branding message. As we crafted this message, we focused on the solutions for his clients; ones that would in turn help *their* clients. Once the message was created, the tactic was to focus on training his entire team on implementation and how it could change the position of the business. We emphasized getting the branding message to prospective and existing clients so that they would know that other services were available. Once we put the branding process in place, the specific tasks and timelines and the communication process began to transform the company from dependency on one product to a full provider of products and services. The new salesperson he had hired embraced the branding message and even though she had little experience, she confidently took the story out on the street. The business got into more case design, and that led to larger profits. Within the first year, the product mix changed dramatically and the company saw a more than 100% increase in their overall business.

SUMMARY: VISION AND BRANDING

- Your vision statement defines where you want your business to go and what you want your business to accomplish.

- Employees cannot adhere to your vision statement if they don't know what it is. Clearly communicate your vision statement to your team so that everyone is moving towards the same goal.

- Your branding message should communicate who you are, what you do, how you do it, and what makes you unique.

- Your vision and brand create the basis for your plan; you cannot develop your plan until you can articulate these elements.

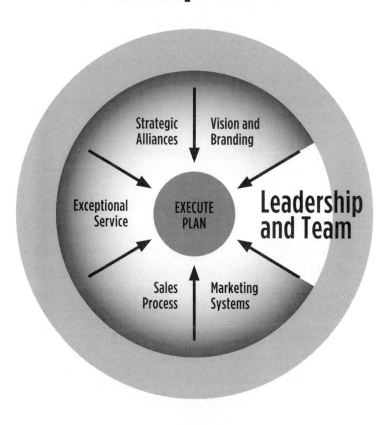

CHAPTER

2

Second Key Element:
Leadership and Team

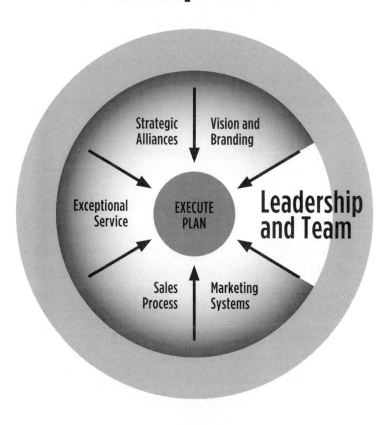

The Challenge: The Funnel at Work

Leadership and management are clearly a vital part of any business. A particular client I worked with had a problem: morale in his company was low and, in addition, he had taken a hands-off management role. His partner handled the managing duties, and his very direct style didn't sit well with some of the employees. To complicate matters, the employees were confused about their roles and responsibilities. The challenge with this client was to define the leadership and build a team that would and could work together to deliver what the partners wanted out of their business. It was a mess, so I ran them through the Second Key Element: Leadership and Team.

What Is Leadership?
Why Is it Important in Your Plan?

In the first chapter you created your vision statement and branding message. The next step is to lead your organization and team toward your vision. Before you do that you need to understand what it takes to be an effective leader and get the most out of your team.

Why does leadership need to be part of your plan? Just as with setting your vision, if you don't identify how you will lead your team toward your vision and goals, it is very difficult to achieve success. I have worked with clients who have a great vision for their organization and a great plan, but fail to progress with either because of lack of leadership. They think that once they have the plan everything else will happen automatically. Six months into their plan, they can't figure out why it's not working.

Leadership is not management. Management is only one component of leadership. Great leaders guide their organizations, teams and visions while constantly striking a balance between coach, cheerleader, disciplinarian and teacher.

Every team has a hierarchy, but the leader—you, the owner—is where the buck stops. Ultimately every final decision, right or wrong, rests on your shoulders. Responsibility for the flow of information to and from your team is yours alone.

In this chapter I will address the following questions and concepts in order to clarify the roles of leader and team, which are of the utmost importance in communicating the positions of all members of your organization. This will help identify their tasks and provide a measure of security so everyone will know exactly what is expected of them.

DEFINING YOUR LEADERSHIP

- How Do You Lead?
- How Is Leadership Addressed in Your Plan?
- Playing to Your Strengths
- *Strengthsfinder*
- Building Your Team and Playing
  to Their Strengths

How Do You Lead?

One of the biggest keys to being a successful leader is to understand your strengths and plan to those strengths. Many of the clients I've worked with have tried to control everything in their organizations and only wind up struggling with their weaknesses.

IT'S A HARD FACT OF LIFE THAT THERE HAVE TO BE LEADERS AND FOLLOWERS AND, PUT SIMPLY, NOT EVERYONE IS CUT OUT TO BE A LEADER.

If you and the other leaders in your team focus on how best you contribute to your organization, and then delegate to the right people the tasks you don't do well or don't enjoy doing, you will have taken a massive step toward giving your organization a chance to succeed. Such delegation is perhaps the essence of sound leadership. Many business owners confuse leadership with management and think they are one and the same; there is nothing farther from the truth. Management is a result of leadership and is only effective if leadership is effective.

A good leader identifies the right people for the various responsibilities involved in running a successful business. Some employees will be assistants to the leader, others' sole tasks will be supply—warehousing, stocking, ordering—and in the middle will be the sales personnel, who may be traveling salespeople or in-house counter service salespeople, depending on the type of business. It's a hard fact of life that there have to be leaders and followers and, put simply, not everyone is cut out to be a leader.

The effective leaders challenge not only their teams but also themselves to keep constantly moving forward. Leadership is critical to the success of your plan—and ultimately the success of your business—because without it your organization is a rudderless ship constantly changing course at the whim of outside influences.

As an effective leader you must determine how to add the strategies that will make you a better leader into your plan. Let's start examining how we can do that.

In his book *Winning*, Jack Welch talks about good leaders. Here are his points as they appear in the *Soundview Executive Summary* (3):

What Leaders Do

1. Leaders relentlessly upgrade their team, using every encounter as an opportunity to evaluate, coach and build self-confidence. *You need to invest the vast majority of your time and energy as a leader in three activities: evaluating, coaching and building the team's self-confidence. Too often, managers think that people development occurs once a year in performance reviews.*

2. Leaders make sure people not only see the vision, they live and breathe it. *As a leader, you have to make the vision come alive. Goals cannot sound noble yet be vague. One of the most common problems in organizations is that leaders communicate the vision to their closest colleagues* *and its implications never filter down to people in front-line positions.*

3. Leaders get into everyone's skin, exuding positive energy and optimism. *An upbeat manager ends up running a team or organization filled with upbeat people. A pessimistic sourpuss somehow ends up with an unhappy tribe all his own.*

4. Leaders establish trust with candor, transparency and credit. *Trust happens when leaders are transparent, candid and keep their word.*

5. Leaders have the courage to make unpopular decisions and gut calls. *Some people long to be loved by everyone. Those behaviors can get you in the soup if you are a leader because there are times you have to make hard decisions—let people go, cut funding to a project or close a plant. A lot has been written about the mystery of gut, but it's really just pattern recognition. Leaders are faced with gut calls all the time, and sometimes the hardest gut calls involve hiring people. However, if you're left with that uh-oh feeling in your stomach, don't hire the guy.*

6. Leaders probe and push with a curiosity that borders on skepticism, making sure their questions are answered with action. *When you're a leader, your job is to have all the questions. You have to be incredibly comfortable looking like the dumbest person in the room.*

Find more tools and resources at www.ultimatebreakthroughplanning.com

7. Leaders inspire risk-taking and learning by setting the example. Winning companies embrace risk-taking and learning. But in reality, these two concepts often get little else than lip service. If you want your people to experiment and expand their minds, set the example yourself. Consider risk-taking.

8. Leaders celebrate. There is not enough celebrating at work—anywhere. Celebrating makes people feel like winners and creates an atmosphere of recognition and positive energy.

How Is Leadership Addressed in Your Plan?

Whether traditional or progressive, every business needs an organizational chart of employees, from the leader down to the administrative and janitorial staff. Each rung of this ladder is of equal importance, and employees need to fully understand their responsibilities and know to whom they report. This should be indicated in the chart. This is sometimes called the "chain of command," a term borrowed from military parlance to indicate how information flows from employer to employee—in both directions, up and down—until it reaches the appropriate level for action on the information.

The organizational chart also serves to indicate how information moves down the chain of command, who is responsible for transmitting order fulfillment to the shipping department, and who is responsible for ordering stock and supplies and entering the information into inventory.

Playing to Your Strengths

Despite the useful idiom, "He who leads least, leads best," there is nevertheless a delicate balance between knowing what is going on at every level of your business and micro-managing (too much supervision and oversight), which robs your employees of initiative and the sense of satisfaction arising from being allowed to do the jobs for which they were hired. Leaders need to know the "big picture" of their operations at all times; they must learn to leave the details—the daily operation—to those they trust and have chosen to do the actual hands-on running of the business. Delegating authority is difficult but necessary.

Wise leaders understand their own areas of expertise and respect those who have different experience and skills. Being able to supplement their own strengths with complementary strengths in their employees is extremely valuable. For instance, if an engineer starts up a company specializing in building bridges, he or she is not likely to have the organizational skills necessary for the day-to-day running of an office and needs office personnel who can assume those duties.

In *The Effective Executive in Action*, management guru Peter Drucker said this about successful leaders:

> *Successful leaders don't start out asking, "What do I want to do?" They ask, "What needs to be done?" Then they ask, "Of those things that would make a difference, which are right for me?" They don't tackle things they aren't good at. They make sure other necessities get done, but not by*

*them; they appoint someone else. Successful leaders make
sure that they are effective. (3)*

Once again—let's hammer it home—the key to being
a successful leader is understanding your strengths and
planning around those strengths. Many of the clients I've
worked with have tried to control everything in their organizations only to wind up exploiting their weaknesses.

StrengthsFinder

Defining your strengths can be difficult at best. One of the
best tools I have found is *StrengthsFinder*, a program developed by the Gallup Organization to provide a way for leaders to identify their management strengths and improve
their areas of weakness through a series of thirty-four
StrengthsFinder themes, including topics such as Activa-
tor, Arranger, Developer, Harmony and Significance. From
their website, www.strengthsfinder.com:

> *Gallup helps organizations capitalize on human talents
> through learning and developmental programs that show
> employees how to develop talents into strengths, then
> apply strengths to build personal and career success.*

The most recent version is *StrengthsFinder 2.0*, by Tom
Rath. This is an extremely helpful tool for determining your
strengths as a leader as well as determining the strengths
of your team. Going through the *StrengthsFinder* exercises
helps you identify your top five strengths. *StrengthsFinder*

2.0 will take you through some of the things you can do to effectively play to those strengths. As Drucker said, "Successful leaders don't do what they aren't good at; they delegate to others" (3). ✳

Other books exist on this subject as well, including *Now, Discover Your Strengths*, by Marcus Buckingham and Donald O. Clifton.

Build Your Team and Play to Their Strengths

In his book *Good to Great*, Jim Collins talks about getting the right people on the bus, getting the wrong people off the bus and getting everyone in their right seats. This is absolutely critical to having a successful business. You must determine who are the right people, and what specific strengths are needed in each position on your team. Getting your team to function effectively is one of the most important aspects of leadership; it goes beyond managing and gets to the core of making sure everyone is on the same page and working toward a common goal.

In Chapter One I talked about creating a vision statement and branding message that need to be lived out in your organization. As the leader of that organization you need to determine what specific things must be done to get your team to act on that vision statement and branding message. If you don't have the right people on the bus, there's a good chance the bus isn't going to go in the right direction.

The first step in getting the right people on the bus is to determine their strengths and how those strengths fit into each team member's position. Unfortunately, most managers manage to minimize people's weaknesses instead of managing to maximize their strengths.

In many of the companies I've worked with you can look at the most successful ones and determine right away that they not only have the right people on the bus but that every member of the team is doing exactly what he or she should be doing. When I take those teams through the *StrengthsFinder* exercise, it ultimately shows that each team member's strengths fit his or her exact position in the company. Conversely, when I work with companies that are struggling and take them through the exercise, I find they either have the wrong people on the bus or they are in the wrong positions; therefore the company is managing to minimize weaknesses versus maximizing strengths. This exercise is a great tool to assess where your team is now and how you can put together a game plan that will get them working effectively.

Communicate Your Plan and Get Buy-In

Once you have determined their strengths, the next challenge is to get your employees functioning as a team. Communicating your vision statement and branding message so that everyone understands clearly where the bus is headed is a critical part of this process; it's the first step in effective team building. The legendary coach of the Green Bay

Packers, Vince Lombardi, said in his book *What It Takes To Be #1*, "A team expresses a coach's personality and its own personality, and this doesn't change from week to week" (55). Your team must understand that first and foremost they need to look at the big picture and keep the bus pointed in the right direction.

UNFORTUNATELY, MOST MANAGERS MANAGE TO MINIMIZE PEOPLE'S WEAKNESSES INSTEAD OF MANAGING TO MAXIMIZE THEIR STRENGTHS.

Putting it All in a Funnel

How do you put leadership and team into a business plan? If we use the Business Funnel Approach we focus first on priorities and then set goals and objectives.

When looking at leadership, look in the mirror: What can make you a more effective leader? What should your priorities be? Maybe it's communicating, playing to your strengths more or delegating more effectively. The more effective your leadership is, the more successful your business will be.

Once you have determined your priorities, goals and objectives, the next step is to identify strategies. When it comes to leadership, a strategy might be to create a better method for communicating, or taking your individual strengths and breaking them down into a method that will help you work more effectively in each area.

Once you have determined two or three strategies to focus on, break down the tools you'll use to get there. Those might be better meetings, a delegation system or specific exercises that will make you a better leader. An excellent resource for exercises is a book called *The Effective Executive in Action*, by Joseph Maciarello, which is a guide based on Peter Drucker's famous book *The Effective Executive*. Maciarello's book takes you through specific exercises that help you focus on the things you need to do to become a better leader. ✳

Once you have identified your priorities for yourself as leader, you need to take your team through the same exercise. One of your first steps should be to take them all through the *StrengthsFinder* exercise as an assessment tool to determine if you have the right people on the bus and whether those people are in the right seats.

Other team priorities to focus on are better communication, more effective meetings and getting everyone on the same page with your vision. Once that is done, you can identify goals and objectives for your team and start identifying strategies to begin implementing.

As in Chapter One, you move through the Business Funnel Approach, breaking down the things that need to happen into specific tasks and timelines and identifying who is responsible for each part of carrying out the plan.

Leadership and team building are critical components in the success of any business and yet traditional business planning models rarely address them. With a steady hand on the wheel and the right people on the bus all working toward a common goal, you give your business the best possibility of success. By breaking down each component through the Business Funnel Approach you will be able to create a process as part of your overall business plan that will help you focus on being a better leader and creating an effective team.

Again in the words of Vince Lombardi, "Leadership is not just one quality, but rather a blend of many qualities; and while no one individual possesses all of the needed talents that go into leadership, each man can develop a combination to make him a leader" (2).

The Answer: The Funnel in Action

The client mentioned at the beginning of this chapter who was experiencing staffing problems because of poor communications and dropping service levels was at first reluctant to do the work necessary to improve things. As I interviewed the owner and staff it became apparent even to them that the lines of communication were terrible, that personnel did not understand their roles and responsibilities, and that everyone was irritated and unhappy. The immediate fix was to make sure that people were in the right positions; therefore, we put everyone through the *StrengthsFinder* exercise to fully understand their attributes so we could switch their positions if necessary. But first I put the leadership team through this exercise so we could develop a communication plan to get the organization back on a success pattern. The immediate finding was that the partners needed to change their leadership style and method of managing. Their communication to their team was poor, and this was the cause of many problems. In addition, through *Strengthsfinder*, we found that some of the employees were in roles that simply did not fit their strengths and so we moved them multiple times in search of something suitable. The next tactic we implemented was a complete review of the communication process, explaining how the passive leadership slowed down the business.

Once we developed specific roles and responsibilities and started putting people in positions where they could succeed, the organization began moving forward again. As for the leadership team, they needed to clearly understand that more active communication had to become part of the company's culture. Several people in key positions needed to be moved because they simply were not making use of their strengths. As the process began to work, employees started to take ownership of their roles and responsibilities, finishing assignments in a timely fashion. The leaders of the company asked for input from employees on productivity. Over the span of about six months the team began to work together with improved results.

SUMMARY: LEADERSHIP AND TEAM

- As the leader of your organization, it is your responsibility to lead your team towards your vision.

- Play to your strengths and the strengths of your team members. It will give all of you a chance to succeed.

- Take your whole team through *StrengthsFinder*. It will help you manage your team in a way that maximizes their strengths rather than minimizing their weaknesses.

CHAPTER

3

Third Key Element:
Marketing Systems

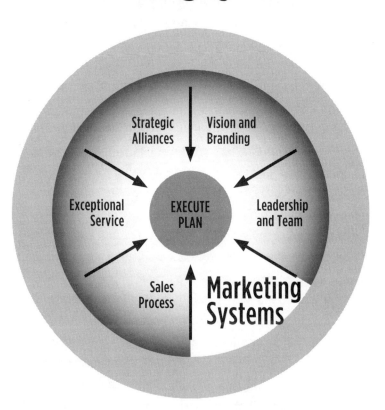

The Challenge: The Funnel at Work

I had a client named Jim who said he was in the marketing business. However, as I began to assess what he actually did, it became clear that he *used to* be in the marketing business but over the years, through sheer laziness, his business had really become a service company. He was in a reactive mode of finding business, not proactive. His marketing ceased to exist and sales flattened out, heading towards decline. When I confronted him, I said, "Jim, you're not a sales and marketing organization anymore. You've become a service organization and if you don't change, your business will continue to decline because you're not adding any new clients or expanding the services of your existing clients."

This brings us to a discussion of marketing systems.

Now that you have a vision statement and branding message and have assessed your leadership and assembled your team, you need to turn your attention to how you will market your products or services. Few products or services are unique. Competition is to be expected, and a marketing system provides the most efficient means of establishing the value of your business to customers. It also provides your employees with a solid process they can follow in reaching the right customers for your product.

The following considerations will help you develop a marketing system. Without a system, your business runs the risk of not bringing your product to the attention of your customers, or of doing so in such a haphazard manner that it will go unnoticed in the competitive marketplace. Increased globalization, technological progress and governmental deregulation demand that your marketing system be both specific to your business and broad enough in appeal and focus to compete in whatever marketplace is appropriate.

A good marketing system goes beyond providing whatever product your business sells; it also creates a demand for the product, and in particular, your brand of the product.

The following sections will help you arrive at an organized markcting system, which can then be put through the Business Funnel Approach.

Why Market?

In the movie *Field of Dreams*, Kevin Costner's character says, "If I build it they will come." Unfortunately business isn't Hollywood. The business owner who thinks that just because he or she has built a better mousetrap, customers will clamber over each other to buy it probably won't be in business long.

No matter what you do, what product you offer, what service you provide—if you don't have a system for letting people know about you, you won't be successful. Developing marketing systems is the Third Key Element in your business plan.

Marketing is not the occasional advertisement, mail

piece or promotion. Creating a marketing system takes into consideration all the possible strategies and tools that are at a marketer's disposal; your plan must incorporate the best and most appropriate strategies for your particular business into a process that is consistent, rational and runs like clockwork.

Dan Kennedy, one of the leading marketing consultants in the country, talks about his big discovery:

> *You must have a reliable, predictable, consistent system that affordably and efficiently provides abundant quantities of quality prospects, customer and clients.* (The Best of Dan Kennedy, 8)

No matter what else you do in your business, if you don't have a system that will drive potential customers to you, it will be very difficult to succeed.

Analyze Where You Are: Identify Priorities

Step one of incorporating a marketing system into your business plan is to fully comprehend your present situation. Maybe you are a great marketer and you just need to formalize your plan, or maybe you do very little marketing and not only do you need to include it into your plan, but you also need to figure out exactly what type of marketing is best for your business.

First, analyze your current marketing situation. Not just "What am I doing?" but also "Do I have a method of measuring success?" A marketing system must be measurable; there is no other way to determine its success or to test various strategies and tools to see which ones are the most successful. Identifying priorities is critical for clarifying the level you need to be at with your marketing and the most important things you need to do to get there.

THERE ARE ONLY THREE WAYS TO GROW YOUR BUSINESS: MORE CUSTOMERS, MORE PURCHASES FROM PRESENT CUSTOMERS AND LARGER PURCHASES FROM ALL CUSTOMERS.

In establishing priorities, examine your present markets and potential customers. What are you already doing for these groups, and what more would you like to be doing? Are there markets you are not addressing but should be?

Go back to the vision statement you created and confirm that what you are trying to accomplish in your business is addressed in your marketing.

Create a Marketing Process:
Set Goals and Objectives

After identifying your priorities, the next step in creating a marketing system is to determine your goals and objectives.

There are only three ways to grow your business: more customers, more purchases from present customers and larger purchases from all customers. With that in mind, clearly determine your goals for marketing.

One of the biggest mistakes business owners make is to launch marketing campaigns without knowing how to measure the success of the campaign. Being able to measure results is critical, so when you set your goals make sure that whatever measurement you use—whether it's sales, customers, transactions, hits on a website—will tie into what you are ultimately trying to accomplish in your marketing.

Define Strategies

Marketing system strategies should be focused around the concept of what your product or service does for your customer.

When I work with financial advisors, I get them to think about what their products do for their clients, not about the products themselves. Too often they are focused on price, product or performance, while their clients are looking for value, solutions and peace of mind. As you define strategies for your marketing systems, think about what your product or service does for your customers.

While working with a community bank, I once asked, "Instead of marketing commercial loans and the best rates, why not market what those loans do for your customers?" The marketing answer is that the loans provide their customers with working capital. So they should think about marketing working capital for business owners, and then package it differently from anyone else—with additional services that provide convenience in using that capital.

Your crucial question before defining strategies should be: How do my customers perceive what I provide to them? Another way to ask that question is: Why do my customers buy from me? What's in it for them?

In marketing systems, the whole idea of "What's in it for my customer?" is absolutely critical. Creating your marketing message is the first step in determining your strategy. The message is critical and should be carried through all of the various tools you use to implement your marketing systems. As you create the message, think about what you intend to accomplish in the minds of your customers, how you want to present your business to them so that they will be encouraged to buy your product or service. Remember to put yourself in their shoes: What's in it for them?

Determine Tools

With marketing systems, your tool kit is only limited by your budget. On the one hand a big, well managed marketing budget will work wonders, but on the other hand, you can have a very successful marketing system using less resources. The advent of the Internet and email permit you to create sophisticated tools at minimal cost. In determining what tools you should use, the first thing to ask is, Is it measurable? Then, Can it be tested? And finally, Can it be targeted? Let's talk about each of those ideas.

Is It Measurable?

When we say *measurable*, we mean being able to determine what the results of the campaign are. For example, is a direct mail campaign measurable? We have the list to which we are mailing, so there is a known number of people who will be getting our piece. Have we created a system for feedback, whether it's calling in or sending something back? Or maybe we have telemarketers call them to follow up? As we create our tools, we want to make sure that what we are creating is measurable.

Can It Be Tested?

The best way to find out if a marketing piece works is to do a couple of versions of it, send it out to small groups and then determine which version gets the greater response.

Can It Be Targeted?

Make sure you are using your marketing tools in the right spots. The best marketers are extremely focused on their message, their market and the medium. The tools they use are tailored to each of those three.

In *The Ultimate Marketing Plan*, Dan Kennedy says this about messaging:

> *Every product, every service, every business either appeals,*
> *or has the potential to appeal, much more strongly to a cer-*

tain definable group of people than it appeals to all people, yet most marketers get to their Grade A prospects only by lucky accident—by throwing out their message to everybody and letting the right people find it. This is like getting a message to your aunt in Pittsburgh by dropping 100,000 copies of your letter out of an airplane as you fly over Pennsylvania. I call this "blind archery." Blindfolded, given an unlimited supply of arrows and some degree of luck, you'll hit the target eventually. (35)

YOUR AVERAGE CUSTOMER MAY TAKE AS MANY AS SEVEN POINTS OF CONTACT BEFORE HE OR SHE IS CONVINCED TO BUY YOUR PRODUCT OR SERVICE.

Put simply, your message must be focused and targeted.

How do you determine what marketing systems and tools you should use? The first thing to remember is to use variety. There are many possibilities:

- Advertising in print and media
- Direct mail
- Signage
- Your website
- Email
- Faxing (though not as useful now because of "Do not fax" lists)

- Statement stuffers

- Newsletters

- Product and service brochures

- Trade shows

- Seminars, conferences and workshops

- Telemarketing

These are some of the tools available to you for your marketing system. By using a variety of methods you can get the best message out to your prospects and customers.

The most critical aspect is to make sure that whatever you're doing is executed consistently. Many business owners start the marketing process, do it for a while, and then quit when they don't see immediate results. Then they say that marketing doesn't work for their business. Your average customer may take as many as seven points of contact before he or she is convinced to buy your product or service. If you stop your marketing at two or three points of contact, your prospect has just moved to your competitor.

Communicate and Train

The next step in developing your marketing system is communicating the game plan to your team and doing the necessary training to implement the strategies and tools you've decided to use.

In communicating the plan to your team, make sure they understand the team priorities and exactly what you are trying to accomplish. Do they understand the targets you are aiming for? In order to bring your team on board, involve them in the next step, tasks and timelines. If you communicate and train before you focus on tasks and timelines, it will make your team feel they have some ownership in this part of the plan.

The training aspect is critical. Make sure the steps you put in place in this section clearly give your team the knowledge and processes they need in order to implement the tools and strategies you have developed. You want to make sure they know how to do what they need to do.

For example, suppose you're planning to use a new email marketing system such as Constant Contact™. In order to execute this part of the plan, someone needs to familiarize him- or herself with how Constant Contact works. By selecting and training that person, you will turn him or her into a valuable resource as it comes time to develop tasks and timelines. Too often business owners cruise on down the marketing path, assuming everyone is following. When they discover no one on their team is able to execute what needs to be done—and they feel as if they have not been part of the decision making process—things get bogged down and eventually grind to a halt, often causing the business to fail.

Create Tasks and Timelines

This is the most crucial part of putting your marketing system into action because here you break down the project into specific tasks. Now the system is implemented. The key is to be as detailed as possible as you start to list the specific things to be accomplished. You should break down each tool into its smallest pieces. What needs to happen in order for each of your tools to be put in place?

For example, if you're going to execute an email campaign, think of each task, step by step:

- Determine which email marketing system to use
- Create the email piece
- Develop your list
- Import the list into your email system
- Import the email marketing piece into your system
- Schedule the email thoughtfully
- Send the email at the right time

Be as detailed as possible. As you break down the campaign into these steps, assign each task to the team member responsible for executing it. Establish a timeline to ensure these tasks are accomplished in the necessary order.

Keep Score and Communicate Results

Once you implement your marketing systems, you need to keep score. As mentioned earlier, you must be able to measure the results to determine whether the various messages and tools are working. The only way to do that is to have a method for keeping score.

- Track the recipients of each piece
- Devise a method for recording their responses
- Determine whether or not you got the results you were seeking

Keeping score is extremely important since it helps establish the degree of success.

If you see a job that is not working, change it. Notice I said "change it," not "stop doing it." Perhaps it's just a matter of tweaking the message or the tool, or maybe it's going to the wrong target. Don't get stuck in the big corporate mentality of "we've executed this and we won't waver from it whether it works or not." Remember the importance of flexibility based on results.

Make sure that everyone on your team knows the results of your marketing campaigns. Getting them involved and informed means they will carry out their functions and take more ownership of the results.

Reward Success

The final piece of your marketing systems is to reward success, not only for your team but also for yourself. When your marketing systems are working efficiently, you will find that is the first step to getting a consistent stream of prospects and customers.

Incorporate rewards into your plan so that when things are progressing as they should, and your team has taken ownership of your marketing systems, there is a dangling carrot constantly out in front of their faces, encouraging increased success in your marketing systems.

Putting it All in a Funnel

You can now create your marketing systems funnel. You know how to let the world—or your target part of the world—know about you and your business. You have cast a net. The next step is to set up a funnel to reel 'em in.

Priorities have been determined, involving where your business is at the moment, where you want it to be and what tools you can use to move it into position.

Your strategies involve various means of marketing your business to your customers and potential customers, informing them of the services or products you offer and why they are superior to the competition.

Tools are the practical means of advertising your business and its services, and there is a wide range of choices available. It's important that, whatever tools you employ, you develop a consistent way of using them, and that the response is measurable.

Your team needs to be fully trained to do their tasks in the overall marketing system, and they need to be kept abreast of responses and shifts in emphasis as you adjust your marketing. Tasks need to be clearly identified and assigned according to the skills of your team members, and a timeline should be drawn up to indicate when each piece of the overall marketing project needs to be completed.

Measuring the success of your marketing is essential to the process of adjusting your approach; you want to spend your marketing budget as efficiently as possible based on return on investment. This information needs to be shared with the members of your team so they know how successful the project is and can offer suggestions for its improvement or expansion.

Rewards need to be earned, and when earned, publicly acknowledged. Marketing is a team effort, and each member of the team shares in the success or failure of your marketing systems.

The Answer: The Funnel in Action

Back to Jim, who thought he had a marketing company but in reality only performed services for his customers. In coaching him, my first and main priority was to get the company marketing again. I got him to visualize his own funnel and what should go into it. He identified three strategies that had to do with the different markets in which his company worked. Those three strategies focused on expanding the scope of products and services to existing clients, then building marketing systems that would attract new clients. We chose three marketing tactics: direct mail, email and educational meetings. These tactics were implemented for both existing and prospective clients, introducing new products and marketing solutions. Next, we created specific tasks and timelines to execute and implement the different marketing strategies. The tasks and timelines were well defined and spread out over a period of six months so that we would have an active marketing calendar. We determined that our goal would be to grow the business 75% in the first year of these marketing initiatives. At the end of the first year it had grown over 60%—not quite the goal but moving in the right direction. More important was the fact that they had opened up a significant number of new relationships that would lead to even more growth in the following years.

SUMMARY: MARKETING SYSTEMS

- Marketing systems are critical to building your brand and telling the world about your business, products, and services.

- There are only three ways to grow your business: find more customers, get more sales from existing customers, or close larger sales from existing customers. Your marketing systems should be hitting each of these segments.

- Remember that your messages should be customer focused. Your messages should tell customers what your product or service can do for them.

- Use a variety of marketing tools in your plan and make sure that each tool can be tested, targeted and measured.

4

Fourth Key Element:
Sales Process

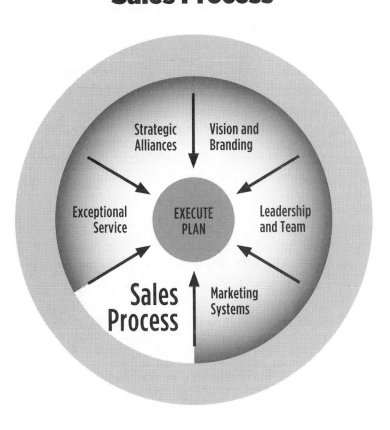

The Challenge: The Funnel at Work

The biggest challenge for many salespeople is understanding their own process and how they work with their clients. I worked with an investment advisor who attended a company-sponsored program that encouraged a wealth management approach. This advisor had created a nice investment management practice, built solely around managing his clients' money, and now the firm was pushing its investment advisors to look at the overall wealth management picture of the clients and offer solutions. The problem for my client was he didn't have a process to help him get started and didn't feel comfortable with the approach the firm recommended. Our challenge was to rebuild his sales process to incorporate wealth management into his business.

In your marketing systems funnel, you built a plan to let the world know about your business, product or service. In your sales process funnel you will determine how to turn potential customers or clients into actual customers or clients. When working with sales organizations I am often amazed at how little thinking they have done about their sales process. Many assume the sale just happens; if

MANY ASSUME THE SALE JUST HAPPENS; IF YOU HAVE THE RIGHT PRODUCT OR SERVICE AND EXPLAIN THE FEATURES AND BENEFITS, THE CUSTOMER WILL BUY. THAT ASSUMPTION LEADS MANY TO BANKRUPTCY.

you have the right product or service and explain the features and benefits, the customer will buy. That assumption leads many to bankruptcy.

First, customers buy based on what they think the product or service will do for them. No matter how many features and benefits it may have, if the concept isn't right for the customers, they won't buy. Your sales process and how well you carry it out will inevitably be a key element in your business success.

What Exactly Is a Sales Process?

A sales process is what happens from the time you contact a prospect—or he or she contacts you—to the time he or she becomes a customer. The period in between—sometimes only a few minutes, sometimes months or years—is a critical time for any business. If you can't turn that prospect into a customer, nothing else you do matters since you won't be around very long.

Marketing Gets Them in the Door, Sales Makes Them Customers

The sales process can take many forms:

- Persuasion over the phone
- Persuasion via a website
- Persuasion in person

- Persuasion through the mail
- Persuasion through a seminar

The better you define your exact sales process—how you turn that prospect into a customer and then a repeat customer—the faster and more successfully your business will grow. Your sales process can be either active or passive, depending on how and what you sell. If you sell products and services that require your salespeople to use a presentation, then your process is very active. If you have a website and your sales process is between your customer and the site, your process is more passive. Even the most passive sales process needs to have structure: you need to understand how your customer buys.

Identify Priorities

The first step in creating your sales process funnel is to identify your sales priorities. In this section you must analyze the current state of your sales process:

- How are you selling your product or service?
- How are your salespeople interacting with your prospects and customers?
- What are you doing for your salespeople to aid in their success?
- Does your sales process fit the vision you've established for your business?
- Does your sale process fit your branding message?

Asking these questions will help identify the priorities for your sales process:

- What can your business do better to sell your product or service?

- How can you make the process faster?

- How can you make it more predictable?

- How can you repeat it?

- What are your priorities?

Setting sales goals and objectives can be difficult. The challenge is not making them so low that they are easily achieved, or so high that they feel unattainable or demoralizing to your sales team.

In determining your priorities, a few things should stand out:

- What is your current sales process—do you sell face-to-face or does your customer buy from you without ever talking to anyone?

- How do your customers buy from you?

- If you sell face-to-face or voice-to-voice (telephone sales), how are you training your personnel so they are in a position to effectively persuade the customer?

- Finally, what makes your product or service unique?

Find more tools and resources at www.ultimatebreakthroughplanning.com

Understand Your Process

Your sales process is how customers interact with you and why they choose you over someone else. One of the key components in understanding your sales process is how your salespeople interact with the customer:

- Do they use features and benefits to sell?

- Do they ask questions?

- Do they present key elements of your product or service?

- Do they diagnose problems well?

In *Exceptional Selling,* Jeff Thull says this about the sales process (paraphrased):

> *In studies of exceptional sales professionals, the number one characteristic they have in common is that they think differently than their less successful colleagues. Their thought processes have far more in common with successful professionals in other disciplines who depend on credible communication than they do with other salespeople. They run a close parallel with the qualities of top leaders: creativity, insight, change management, integrity and respect. Awareness is the first step in the process of selling. For example, the compulsion to have an immediate answer for everything creates a significant barrier to listening and understanding customers' situations. The more effective we become as a decision-process guide, the more likely customers are to reveal the privileged information we need to execute successfully. (53–54)*

After you understand exactly how your salespeople interact with your prospects and customers and how your customers buy, the next thing you must understand is why your customers buy your product or service.

In my experience working with salespeople, I find they get too involved in the discussion of features and benefits and forget that customers buy a product or service based on what they think it will do for them, not on what the salesperson promises.

I recently worked with some realtors whose sales sheets had pictures and all the hard data on each home, but they forgot a key component: they didn't paint a picture in the buyer's mind; they didn't sell the concept versus the product. What they should have said was that the house has a handsome deck on the back overlooking a wooded area; a beautiful place to sit, relax and have a glass of wine after a long day at work. This statement encourages buyers to visualize themselves living in the house, rather than just providing facts and figures about the house.

How your sales process distinguishes you from your competitors can be of primary importance in the success of your business. Therefore, your understanding of your sales process is a key priority in the Business Funnel Approach.

Set Goals and Objectives

In this step, you set goals and objectives for your sales process. Focus on your sales goals as well as the goals for making the sales process more successful. Here you should look not only at your sales results, but also at the specific steps that will make your salespeople more successful:

- Prospecting
- Sales calls
- Presentations
- Learning your sales process

Customers: Your Greatest Asset

In considering goals and objectives the one thing many businesses miss is their greatest asset: their current customer base. It is much easier to sell to an existing customer than to try to find new customers. Is your business set up to capitalize on your current customer base? Are there opportunities for your satisfied customers to buy from you again? Are you incorporating that into your sales process and your goals?

I'll reiterate: There are three basic ways to grow your business: more customers, more sales from existing customers and larger sales from existing customers. Your goals should focus on all three of these areas. How you capitalize on your greatest asset will determine your success.

IT IS MUCH EASIER TO SELL TO AN EXISTING CUSTOMER THAN TO TRY TO FIND NEW CUSTOMERS.

Define Strategies

In defining strategies, begin by looking at your sales process and analyzing how your customer buys from you. If you use salespeople, how are they interacting with the customer and what are they doing—both good and bad—to make or break the sale? Defining your sales strategy means looking at how you can make your sales process more successful, and how that process can be developed with your salespeople. In the event you don't have salespeople, how does your customer buy from you and what could make that process more successful?

Try Diverse Processes

One method of creating a stronger sales process is to diversify how you sell. As in your marketing systems, how can your sales process be varied and broadened so your sales are not tied to just one method? Maybe you have salespeople in the field but haven't developed a means of additional, direct sales through the Internet.

Consider add-on sales. In a project I worked on for a major insurance company, they had a sales force selling face-to-face, concentrating on a specific product. We created a direct sales campaign that followed up the face-to-face sales by adding an additional product the existing customer might need. This expansion gave the company another significant revenue stream and tapped into their greatest asset, their existing customers. With this "back-end" sale, we increased the number of sales per customer.

Your strategies should not only strengthen your sales process, but also motivate and invigorate your salespeople. A strategy that you can use is to create a formal sales process for your salespeople; a track to run on. In his book *No B.S. Sales Success*, Dan Kennedy, a top sales and marketing guru, describes the sales process in six steps (140):

1. *Get permission to sell*

2. *Design an offer*

3. *Deliver a structured presentation*

4. *Use emotional logic*

5. *Close the sale*

6. *The morning after*

This takes your salespeople through each step of the process, formalizing it so that each salesperson is doing exactly the same thing and delivering the same message.

Determine Tools

What specific tools are necessary to advance your strategies? These could be:

- New presentation materials
- New customer discovery materials
- Different sales scripts
- Better interactive web sales tools
- Generally better sales tools

In determining what tools you should focus on, try to limit their number to no more than four. More than that tends to spread you too thin and confuses your sales team. Let's take a look at two sales tools: conceptual selling and sales presentations.

Conceptual Selling

In considering tools to increase sales, keep in mind the idea of conceptual selling. Remember, as mentioned earlier, customers buy for their own reasons, not yours. In order to create a more successful sales process you need to determine what those reasons are and have your sales team focus on them. A product sale always follows the concept sale. In the example of the realtors painting a picture of living in a house for their potential buyers, they used flyers with concepts their buyers could relate to such as comfort, convenience, location, style and leisure. They were trying to get potential buyers to imagine actually living in that house and how it would feel.

As you examine your sales process for conceptual selling, create key questions to determine what concepts appeal to your potential customers. These should be the kinds of questions that generate emotional responses. Good questions to ask are: How do you feel about this product or service? What do you think about this product or service? The questions should generate statements from customers about how the concept of the sale pertains to them. Each customer will have a different take on the concept and how it fits his or her needs.

Sales Presentations

Improving presentations for your sales team or your interactive sales process will have an immediate effect on your sell rate.

Todd Duncan, author of *High Trust Selling*, says this about presentations:

> *The Presentation is about offering captivating, fulfilling solutions to your prospects in order to secure their devoted business. A poor presentation can quickly make a prospect disappear. That's why making an early impact is so critical. The truth is that prospects actually close their own sales if you offer valuable solutions to their real needs and values. (192)*

Communicate and Train

The next step in your sales process funnel is to communicate with and train your team. First bring your whole team into the sales process whether they are directly involved in sales or not. Make sure everyone on your team understands your sales process, and they will support your sales process more effectively. The training piece you devise will vary based on what each individual's role will be. For your direct salespeople, their training may already be part of your strategies since the goal should always be to increase their effectiveness.

Create Tasks and Timelines

You will achieve success in this area of your plan by breaking each tool into specific tasks and timelines. If you have decided you need a better sales presentation, then some of your tasks and timelines need to be:

- Evaluate your current sales presentations and determine what you will keep and what you will change
- Design a new presentation and supporting materials
- Train your team on the presentation
- Have your team practice the presentation and start using it

Assigning each task to a responsible person, along with a specific timeline, will keep the project on task. As I said earlier, you want to be as specific as possible and break down each tool to the smallest possible task and assign a deadline for getting that task done.

Keep Score and Communicate Results

One of the most important points in the sales process is keeping score. You should be less concerned with actual sales than with your methods and the activities of your salespeople. Your scorekeeping system should focus on the specific activities you want your salespeople or process to accomplish. For instance, how many calls, appointments, presentations and referrals are they making? How many sales are coming through your website? How many direct sales letters are going out and how many responses are we receiving? These are the things your salespeople should be tracking.

Keeping score on a weekly and monthly basis helps to determine what specific things are working, why one salesperson is outperforming another, and what you need to change in your sales process to get a better response. You can further improve your process by continually monitoring it, which will directly improve your sales.

Reward Success

The last step is rewarding success. This is critical with salespeople since you want to consistently give them reasons to achieve. To attract and retain the best salespeople, offer the best compensation package based on performance and reward achievement with incentives. You need to hire the right people, ones who are driven to succeed. As Todd Duncan says in *High Trust Selling:*

> *The fact is if you don't have an effective, efficient plan for selling, any business you get is accidental. The key is to have a plan that generates the right kind of sales, from the right kind of accounts, backed by the right sales process, which produces the maximum revenue for your time. (52)*

Your sales process funnel will help your organization become more successful. Whether you sell actively or passively, you must first understand your process and then fine-tune it for maximum results. Your business doesn't exist without selling something!

The Answer: The Funnel in Action

The usual problem with investment advisors is that they have been so intent on providing investment solutions over the years that they lose money by not taking a more holistic approach to their sale process, and certainly the client I introduced at the beginning of this chapter was no different. The first thing we needed to do was analyze his existing book of clients and the types of products they bought from him. As we went through this exercise it became apparent that his sales process needed to be revised to take full advantage of what he could provide for his clients. As we set strategies, we looked at some concepts that he was not currently utilizing. We started off with simple concepts with which he could easily become familiar, along with readily available resources that he could gradually incorporate into his sales process—rather than suddenly trying to provide everything. Our strategies incorporated these concepts into his fact-finding and sales presentations so he could become more comfortable conversing about them with clients. Tasks and timelines included developing scripts and support materials. After the first year he increased his company's revenue over 200% without working any harder.

He was also now in a position to be more selective about the people with whom he worked.

SUMMARY: SALES PROCESS

- Your sales process is what happens from the time you contact a prospect (or he or she contacts you) to the time he or she becomes a customer.

- The more you can define your sales process, the more repeatable and successful it will be.

- Train your sales people to use a variety of sales tools.

- Reward your salespeople. It will help you attract and retain an effective sales force.

Fifth Key Element:
Exceptional Service

The Challenge: The Funnel at Work

Service is always in the eye of the beholder and most business owners think their service is pretty good. A client who had been in business for a long time felt that because he had very little turnover in staff and service stayed consistent, he was doing well. However, as I began to interview his staff and some of his customers, it became quite evident that in reality the service team had become complacent. In this case, time had passed them by; they were not utilizing new technology. In reality, the level of service *had* dropped below expected standards. The problem was that no one, including the owner, had noticed.

The quality of service can make or break any business. There is a huge difference between delivering good service and delivering exceptional service. Many businesses brag that they deliver good service, and it seems a given that if you deliver bad service you'll never stay in business. But very few businesses can deliver truly exceptional service.

What Is Exceptional Service?

Before you can build in a process for delivering exceptional service you must understand what exceptional service is.

- Exceptional service makes your customers say "Wow"
- Exceptional service goes beyond what is expected
- Exceptional service can be the best sales and marketing tool you have

Exceptional service creates what Ken Blanchard calls "raving fans" because it anticipates what customers are looking for and delivers more than they expect. Exceptional service provides customer experiences that cause customers to come back for more.

When it comes to delivering exceptional service, the first step is to make sure you are already delivering good service. It's virtually impossible to go from bad service to exceptional service. It takes time to get your team to understand what it takes to deliver good service and then move them to the next level of delivering exceptional service. One of the easiest ways to make your team aware of good service is to put them in their customer's shoes: if they were purchasing your product, what type of service would they expect?

Service and Vision

In order to move up to delivering exceptional service, you need to make sure that what you are trying to do in terms of service matches the description of your vision. Whether you are trying to be the best, fastest, most responsive, most caring—whatever your vision—you need to follow through in your service. Your service must mirror what you want your company to be and where it should go. It is also important to understand that the quality of service can color customers' perceptions and will go a long way in determining the effectiveness of your service. One slip-up and the perception of that customer can have a lasting effect on how your business is characterized, and that one customer's perception spreads to other potential customers. Do you have to be perfect? No. Everyone occasionally makes mistakes, but when it happens, the manner in which you respond to that customer or potential customer goes a long way in determining his or her opinion of your business and your service.

Identify Priorities

The first step in creating your service funnel is to look at the ways you currently interact with your customers and determine what is working well and what isn't. In the words of Jim Collins, "You must confront the brutal facts." No matter how bad the result, this is the first step in committing to deliver exceptional service.

Perception Turns into Reality

In his book *Broken Windows, Broken Business*, Michael Levine talks about the impact of perception on a business:

> *In business perception is even more critical. The way a customer or potential customer perceives your business is a crucial element in your success or failure. Make one mistake, have one rude employee, let one customer walk away with a negative experience one time and you are inviting*

disaster. Perception is also something that happens in the blink of an eye. There is nothing more fleeting than a first impression; it is made in a heartbeat. But a perception can be made at anytime, even after you have been acquainted with a person or company for years. And opinions turn on such perceptions. For example, let's say you have bought your coffee at the same store every day for the past five years on your way to work in the morning. You've gone there unfailingly, sometimes added a bagel or muffin and occasionally stopped in at lunchtime. The counter staff knows your name, knows your usual order, and can antic-ipate your preferences. But one day, even without thinking about it, you happen to notice as you stand in line wait-ing to order that the walls haven't been painted in years. There are slight cracks and chips in the paint just behind the counter help. It's never occurred to you before, but that small perception makes a difference. Maybe you start to wonder if those paint chips aren't falling into the coffee or onto a surface where rolls and bagels are cut and pre-pared for sale. Perhaps the fact that you noticed the paint job makes you realize how long you've been waiting in line every morning. That one little perception can pack an extraordinary wallop, can't it? (5)

In determining priorities, focus on the small things that can add up to big things; make sure that the old adage "under-promise and over-deliver" is a part of your process for creating exceptional service.

Your priorities should focus on how you deliver your

vision to your customers and how you can transform those customers to "raving fans." You need to think about how you can turn service into a real sales and marketing tool that can help you grow your business significantly. Taking your service to the next level, anticipating what your customers want and then delivering more, is what you want to shoot for. So in setting your priorities, think about a few things that you can begin to work on to turn service into a key element in your business.

Set Goals and Objectives

In setting goals and objectives for your service, you need to create service standards. Basically, these standards are what must be met each time a customer does business with you. Your written service standards should be the very minimum conventional expectations your customers have of you. You want to be seen exceeding these standards!

What ought to be included in written service standards? Each business is different, but the following list is a good place to start no matter what your business. Your service standards should include:

- Your response time to customer inquiries
- Your turnaround time in delivering goods or services
- Your return/refund policy
- The method with which you greet customers
- Your expectations of employees in dealing with customers

- Your follow-up on orders or purchases
- How you deliver bad news to customers

If you have already addressed these areas as part of developing your goals and objectives, then you've made a good start on putting written service standards into place and getting your team to understand exactly what they are and how to meet them.

Define Strategies

To start delivering exceptional service, we come back to the mainstay of putting yourself in your customers' shoes. You then determine why they buy from you, what they expect, and whether or not you foster an experience that will cause them to tell someone else about your business. These considerations should already be part of your earlier funnels.

Create Client Experiences

One of the best current business stories is how Howard Schultz built Starbucks on the whole idea of client experience. In my workshops I often ask, "What does Starbucks sell?" The answer is always "Coffee." My response to that is if Starbucks just sold coffee at $3.00 a cup they would have gone out of business a long time ago. Starbucks sells a customer experience, and the way they deliver that experience has made them the success they are. Starbucks wants you to stay in their shops and have a meeting, read the newspaper or work on your computer, and they have created an atmosphere that invites you not only to stay, but to keep coming back. Jim Alling, President of Starbucks, U.S., says in the foreword of Joseph Michelli's *The Starbucks Experience*:

> One of the ways in which we express the nature of what it means to be a Starbucks partner is through the Green Apron Book. It's a pocket sized book that puts into words some of the core "ways of being" that you need in order to be successful at Starbucks. They are to be welcoming, be genuine, be knowledgeable, be considerate, and be involved. They are simple words, and they distill everything you need to know about Starbucks and the people who work here.

Starbucks understands that the first step in creating client experiences is to create employee experiences. They go out of their way to embrace, train and reward employees to ensure a total buy-in, which is a great springboard to creating client experiences. In *The Starbucks Experience*, Michelli identifies five key business principles that drive its success (16):

- *Make it Your Own*
- *Everything Matters*
- *Surprise and Delight*
- *Embrace Resistance*
- *Leave Your Mark*

These five principles can be the key strategies in any successful mission to deliver exceptional service. Let's expand on each of these ideas:

- *Make it Your Own:* By allowing your team to take ownership of the decisions they make relating to service, you free them up to do what they feel is right for the customer.

- *Everything Matters:* By paying attention to all the little details, you create the perception that you are a well-oiled machine designed specifically for your customer.

- *Surprise and Delight:* By offering surprise and delight you constantly give your customers more than they expect.

- *Embrace Resistance:* By embracing resistance you make sure that when things don't go right, not only will you take care of that customer, but you and your team will learn from what went wrong.

- *Leave Your Mark:* By leaving your mark you leave an indelible imprint in you customers' minds that will not only bring them back, but will have them telling others about their experience.

The strategies you choose as part of your plan to deliver exceptional service start with creating client experiences. Remember, these don't have to be big, expensive strategies; they can be as simple as the manner in which you answer your phone.

Determine Tools

In determining your tools, look at the specific things you can do to deliver exceptional service. We have discussed strategies and some of the things you might want to do to start delivering exceptional service. Now we want to get more specific. Remember: don't try and do it all at once. You need to take small steps to get where you want to be.

In his book *Raving Fans*, Ken Blanchard looks at creating a method for getting to the point of being able to create "raving fans." He talks about delivering "plus one," and advises:

> *Improve by one percent a week, and you improve more than 50%. If you try and do too much at once, it is likely that you will fail to deliver consistently. At the least you'll feel frustrated or overwhelmed by the enormity of the job ahead. If you improve by one percent each week, you feel confident you can do the job. By the end of the year, you have improved your product or service by more than 50%.* (117)

In determining the specific tools, look at your written service standards and figure out what things you and your team can do to carry out those standards. What specific activities can you do to empower your team to take ownership of customer situations, to surprise and delight customers or make sure that everything matters? There is no single right answer; it all goes back to how you're delivering your service now, and what you need to do to take it to a higher level. By choosing specific things to focus on, you will begin to create an environment where you can deliver exceptional service.

Communicate and Train

This piece is probably the most critical in this chapter. Your team not only needs to be on the same page, but they need to understand that each and every one of their actions affects the customers' perceptions. You probably don't have a *Green Apron Book* like Starbucks, but it is vital to create your own vision and message about what you want your business to deliver when it comes to service and client experiences. In communicating your message, make sure that everyone on your team understands how important this is and what is at stake. To enforce the message you must train your team to deliver exceptional service and teach them how to create client experiences.

They need to be involved in the process. Many of your team members are going to have direct contact with your customers or be involved in delivering your products or services. Getting their input and assistance in creating your written service standards—and how you will execute—is critical. Your service is only as good as your weakest team member.

Create Tasks and Timelines

Start by breaking down the specific things your team will do to create client experiences and deliver exceptional service. As mentioned earlier, don't try to do it all at once. Create your tasks and timelines slowly over a period of time so that, as Ken Blanchard says, you begin improving by one percent a week. In developing tasks and timelines, make sure you assign the tasks in each area of service to those team members who will be directly involved, and hold them accountable to the timelines you have established.

For example, if you are going to focus on the smallest details of your business, the specific tasks may be something as simple as cleaning up customer areas. Who will do it and when and how often it will get done go into your tasks and timelines.

In implementing particular service standards such as faster delivery time, what specific things have to happen to speed up your delivery? The more specific you get, the better.

Keep Score and Communicate Results

Use this part of the delivering exceptional service funnel to determine whether your entire team is on the same page. Put systems into place that will allow you to keep score. It could be as simple as tracking delivery, customer response, customer surveys, or any tools that enable you to determine whether you are meeting your service standards. These systems will tell you whether or not you're delivering exceptional service and will help you to see if you need to put into place methods to help you incrementally improve your service. Now communicate these results to your team so that they will know how they are doing and what you are trying to accomplish.

Reward Success

Celebrating success is important for developing company morale. As your team understands and accomplishes the objectives of delivering exceptional service, they will begin to collect service success stories. Those stories need to be shared and celebrated. Individual achievements as well as team achievements should be rewarded. This can be done simply at the time they happen, but should also be repeated with the entire team present to reinforce what you are trying to accomplish in delivering exceptional service and encourage everyone on the team to try harder to match the best.

Delivering exceptional service is a way to clearly differentiate yourself from your competitors. Most customers expect good service and bad service can be the death of your business. Delivering exceptional service takes you to a higher level by anticipating what your customers want and providing even more than they expect. Exceptional service can do more for the growth of your company than any marketing or sales initiative.

The Answer: The Funnel in Action

It proved quite difficult to get the client mentioned at the beginning of this chapter to acknowledge that he had been left behind by changing technology and that there indeed was a problem. Some people have to be dragged kicking and screaming to success. Once I convinced him that his entire business looked a little antique, the penny dropped and his priorities became clear: Fix it, and take the opportunity to create raving fans. The strategy that we settled on was to look over the company's service processes, utilizing all the existing technology to deliver the results we wanted. Our strategies were to look at each area of service and determine one thing in each area that could be improved. As we went through the exercise it became evident that the people responsible for delivering the service had never been asked what could be improved. The team started coming back with great ideas for improving each area. These ideas were prioritized to determine which ones could be implemented immediately, which ones would take more time and which ones couldn't be done. The tasks and timelines were created from this list. Each week the team delivered a progress report. Each new idea had specific measurements attached so we could track effectiveness. Six months later I talked with some of the customers and verified a substantial change in their perception of the service being delivered. In addition, the team had a sense of ownership in their exceptional service and took pride in creating raving fans.

SUMMARY: EXCEPTIONAL SERVICE

- Your service should mirror your vision of what you want your company to be.

- In conjunction with your team, focus on how to create positive client experiences. This helps everyone understand how actions affect customer perceptions.

- Don't try to dramatically change your level of service overnight. If you improve by one percent every week, you will have improved your service by more than 50 percent at the end of the year.

Find more tools and resources at www.ultimatebreakthroughplanning.com

6

Sixth Key Element:
Strategic Alliances

The Challenge: The Funnel at Work

One of the best ways to grow your business is to find strategic alliances that can help you do things that aren't your strengths. These alliances can expose your business to new markets, products and services. My client in Charlotte understands this better than most business owners. Over the past few years, he and his wife and their team have identified several areas that they don't do well. The challenge with any of my clients is to first get them to admit that they need help and then open up to the possibilities of strategic alliances.

The final element of your business plan is to create strategic alliances in areas that can help you grow your business. Ask yourself these two questions:

- What don't I do well or don't like to do that someone else could be doing?

- What relationships can I strike up that will help my business grow?

These questions are the basis for any strategic alliances you create. They will help you determine what is best for you and your business. How you leverage these strategic alliances will greatly affect how you grow your business.

What Am I Doing That Someone Else Could Do More Effectively?

During the start-up phase, most business owners have a tendency to try and do everything. Shortly into the venture they discover that trying to keep all the balls in the air at once is virtually impossible. Things start to slip through the cracks, and the next thing you know you're behind in the areas you don't like to do or that fall outside your strengths. In order to operate at maximum efficiency you must be able to focus on what you do well and let someone else do the things you don't do well. As we discussed in the chapter on leadership, this may simply mean delegating it to someone in your organization who is capable. Or it may mean finding capable people outside the organization and forming an alliance with them. This kind of outsourcing is very common and very helpful.

What Strategic Alliances Can I Form to Grow My Business?

You need to figure out what relationships can help you grow your business. How can you partner with other businesses or people who can help you develop existing markets or expand into new ones? You can also think about how you could add new revenue streams that don't necessarily come from your existing products or services. Are there relationships that you can create that are win-

win situations for both parties and can add new revenue streams?

Copy this and tape it to your computer screen:

- What relationships would help my business grow?

- Who can help me develop existing markets or expand into new ones?

- How do I add new revenue streams that don't originate in my existing business?

- Can I foster win-win situations with potential partners to create new revenue streams?

Identify Priorities

When laying out your priorities, look at those areas that are critical to the ongoing success of your business from an operational standpoint, as well as from a new market and revenue standpoint. What operational areas of your business could use strategic alliances?

Accounting and Legal

These are two areas where you should always rely on strategic alliances unless you have specific expertise. In deciding with whom to work, create a specific list of what you need in each of these areas: documents drafted, bookkeeping services, tax work, etc. There is a broad range of services available, from inexpensive to very expensive. Pick the people that understand your type of business and have other clients who are of a similar size to your company.

Marketing

If you don't have marketing expertise, find someone who does. This is crucial to the success of your business, so don't take a chance on doing it badly. Make sure you have someone you can bounce ideas off of and who can assist you in developing marketing strategies to take your business to the highest levels. In my work with brokerage agencies I find that many of my clients have some ideas on what they would like to do but have no idea how to execute them, so they rely on their insurance carriers for their marketing. That results in limited product and sales ideas, and will never help them create their own branding.

Strategic Planning

This is one area many business owners completely ignore. Yet, as this book attests, it is one of the most important areas for creating a successful business. Having someone who can assist you in clarifying your vision of where you want to go and how to get there is important.

Technology

Except for tech companies, this is one area in which I think all businesses seek outside help. Technology in business today is so critical that if you don't get things set up right from the start you can have very costly problems in the future. It is also important to have someone who can keep your systems functioning optimally and keep them upgraded. A good tech alliance can also show you ways to more effectively run and market your business using the latest technology. This alliance is worth its weight in gold. Be cautious, because you want to tell them exactly what you're looking for. Have them tell you exactly what they will do for you and how much it will cost. I have had many clients who have been drawn into technology alliances that wound up doing nothing but costing them money.

Administrative

If you are a small business and you don't want to hire a big administrative staff, one of the best things you can do is to consider outsourcing administrative help. Good administrative help is difficult to find these days, and an option is to look at outside services such as secretarial staffing, direct mailing firms, etc., to help you get those mundane, daily administrative tasks done. This frees up your time to do what you do best. One great resource that I have found for my business is a virtual assistant. Today's technology enables your assistant to be located anywhere; there is an association of virtual assistants (www.virtualassistants.com) that can provide you with many administrative options. ✳

In defining priorities for strategic alliances to help your business grow, you should consider:

Resources

What types of individuals or companies can provide you with expertise that will make your product or service more likely to be purchased by your customers? For example, I help community banks develop relationships with outside vendors that can give them expertise in insurance and investments. These are areas that community banks need to be offering to their customers to generate fee income, but typically they don't have the necessary expertise. This is an example of adding a resource that gives them expertise and creates a win-win situation.

Networks

Affiliating with networks or organizations that are either in the same business or have some common ground opens your business to additional resources and possible marketing opportunities. These networks may offer access to more products, more revenue opportunities, or more markets. In many cases they can be an excellent place to form strategic alliances.

Partnerships

Creating strategic partnerships can be a great way to build additional revenue streams. These partnerships must benefit all parties. Things like affiliate programs, joint ventures and partnerships can be a great way to expand your business and open up new markets and revenue streams.

Set Goals and Objectives

It is extremely important in determining goals and objectives to set clear timelines for what activities and events will happen as a result of your strategic alliances. As you establish these relationships, you'll want to set clear objectives for all parties concerned. In some cases you will be able to project specific revenue.

Define Strategies

Ask this simple question: What am I trying to accomplish with this strategic alliance? Your strategies should revolve around this question. If you're developing an alliance with a marketing firm, what specific strategies can it provide to help you with your marketing? It could be creating better marketing communications, direct mail programs, or a more effective online presence. Whatever it is, identify the specific things you will do to maximize that relationship.

When I first started using a virtual assistant, I made a list of specific things my assistant could help me with that I didn't enjoy doing but were important to my business. One of the first things we worked on was updating my database for marketing. I had been putting it off for a long time, but it was a critical task tied into my marketing strategies.

By determining exactly what you are trying to accomplish and tying it into your strategic alliances, you will begin to define your strategies.

Determine Tools

In this section we examine how you will set up these strategic alliances. Will they be set up formally or informally? How will they function?

Set Up the Relationship

The first step in setting up a strategic alliance is to determine who is going to do what. What specific roles and responsibilities exist between each party? The sooner you get this clarified, the sooner your alliance will be successful. Defining your responsibilities and the other party's responsibilities will keep the relationship from moving laterally and give it the best chance for success. How you set up the relationship will depend on the relationship itself. If it is a formal relationship, there should probably be a contract or written agreement that outlines specifically each party's roles and responsibilities with guidelines for reviewing whether the relationship is working. Depending on how comfortable you are with the formal relationship or informal arrangement, you should still sit down and outline the expectations of each side, how you will determine whether or not it is working and how often you will review the results.

AN EXIT CLAUSE SHOULD BE AGREED UPON IN CASE THE ALLIANCE DOESN'T WORK, AND A RENEWAL CLAUSE IN CASE IT DOES.

An exit clause should be agreed upon in case the alliance doesn't work, and a renewal clause in case it does. The more these things are covered on the front end, the better the chance of the relationship succeeding. Even in something as apparently simple as working with a CPA, the expectations should be laid out up front. Will he or she just prepare your tax returns, or do you expect him or her to do tax planning as well? There is a big difference, and making sure everyone knows who is responsible for what from the beginning is vital.

Execute the Alliance

Once you have created the alliance, getting it up and running is next. Communication is crucial, especially in the early stages of the arrangement, so that everyone stays on the same page. Regular meetings or conference calls can help catch potential problems in the relationship that could sidetrack it and keep everyone on point with their roles and responsibilities. As the relationship evolves, constant review and continual improvement will make it a viable, profitable relationship.

Communicate and Train

One of the challenges in communicating and training is to make sure your team understands your alliances, so that they are being utilized and no one is duplicating tasks. Bring your team together and educate them on why you have created the strategic alliance. Whether it is to be more efficient or to help grow your business, your team needs to understand there is a very clear purpose in creating the alliance. Then you need to educate them about how the relationship will work, and what are the roles and responsibilities of each partner. If your team will need to either stop doing something or do it differently because of a strategic alliance, make sure that they can adjust so that the relationship will work for all involved.

I have worked with clients who have set up arrangements, but their staff can't let go of specific tasks. There are two problems with that: first, they are duplicating efforts; and second, they become less efficient. The alliance is no longer working the way it was intended.

Create Tasks and Timelines

Tasks and timelines go back to roles and responsibilities. Setting up clear, detailed tasks for each party helps create a successful relationship. Once those tasks have been assigned, create specific timelines to which each party

STRATEGIC ALLIANCES CAN TAKE EVEN THE BEST BUSINESSES TO HIGHER LEVELS, BUT IF YOU DON'T FOCUS ON THEM AS PART OF YOUR PLAN AND FIND WAYS TO INCORPORATE THEM, YOU WILL ONLY COME UPON THEM BY ACCIDENT OR THROUGH TRYING TO GET SOMETHING DONE IN TIMES OF PANIC.

must adhere. The review and communication process must keep these tasks and timelines in mind and make sure that things are happening in the way both parties wanted.

Keep Score and Communicate Results

The review process is based on specific things that should be happening in order for the relationship to work. If you are setting up an administrative relationship, are things getting done in a timely manner, and is the quality of work being done to your satisfaction? And are the materials necessary for completing administrative tasks getting to your administrative person in a timely manner? In a relationship that is meant to add new markets or revenue, are the specific goals for sales, revenue and new customers being met, and is the strategic alliance creating a win-win situation for both sides?

Reward Success

The best reward for success is to maintain the strategic alliance and continually find ways to expand it. The best strategic alliances I've seen don't need to be rewarded for success because it happens on both sides and creates a positive situation that makes employees want to keep working and expanding.

Most strategic alliances happen by accident, not by design, when business owners become desperate to find new ways to do things. But by adding strategic alliances into the mix of your business plan and thinking about how they can specifically help you run and grow your business, you can proactively search out possible relationships that will help you accomplish the things that you either can't or don't like to do, or new ways to generate new markets and new revenue streams. Strategic alliances can take even the best businesses to higher levels, but if you don't focus on them as part of your plan and find ways to incorporate them, you will only come upon them by accident or through trying to get something done in times of panic.

The Answer: The Funnel in Action

I asked my clients in Charlotte to identify ways they might grow their business outside their comfort zone. Their first issue was discomfort with new technology. Second, we identified a possible new revenue source to be explored, one that my clients were not sure how to approach. After brainstorming about possible strategies, we decided upon two. To address the technology issue, we found a technology support provider to work with them. Our strategy for the new revenue source was entirely outside the box: We created a completely new company to explore new revenue areas that fell outside the existing company. Now, this wasn't what I would call a typical strategic alliance; however, because we brought in someone else to build it, the new company became a sort of customized strategic alliance.

In determining the specific tools, we focused on what the technology provider could do and what we needed done—nothing else. The specific tasks and timelines were then broken down into who would do what and when it would be done. As we got into the key milestones we focused on timelines and what we needed to measure to determine success. In the end the technology provider turned into a valuable resource that to this day provides all the technology support the company needs. And, the new company we created turned out to be a viable revenue source that opened up markets and opportunities for the owners.

SUMMARY: STRATEGIC ALLIANCES

- Strategic alliances should help you grow your business and complete business functions that you can't or don't want to perform.

- In the event that your strategic alliance doesn't work out, make sure that you have and understand your exit strategy.

- Communication with both your team and your partners is critical to the success of your strategic alliance.

7

Create and Execute Your Plan

Identify Priorities
Set Goals and Objectives
Define Your Strategies
Determine Your Tools
Communicate and Train
Create Tasks and Timelines
Keep Score and Communicate Results
Reward Success

We have now covered the Six Key Elements of business success:

- Vision and Branding
- Leadership and Team
- Marketing Systems
- Sales Process
- Exceptional Service
- Strategic Alliances

As we covered these areas, we discussed how you apply the Business Planning Funnel to each element. Now it's time to create an overall game plan and execute that plan. Your plan may include all six areas, or it may incorporate certain parts of a few of them. There is no right or wrong answer.

Let's look at how you put your plan together.

Timing

Most business plans look ahead one to seven years. I don't believe such a long time frame works for most businesses. I suggest you create a plan that focuses on the next six months. This gives you enough time to implement the strategies you have chosen to try, but also allows you to assess where your business is now, how it might need to be changed and how different priorities and strategies may need to be implemented during the next six months.

I believe that most businesses can experience distinct changes over a six-month period—let alone a year or longer. By creating a six-month plan you have the capability to make adjustments as changes occur in your business, market and industry.

Identify Priorities

We've identified priorities in each of the Six Key Elements. Now it's time to boil those priorities down to the three or four most important ones. As you look at the priorities you've identified in each area, think about which ones have the most impact on your business right now. Which are the most critical to get your business on track and growing to where you want it to be? Is it better marketing, better service, better communication with your team, better sales processes, better vision and branding?

If you have not gone through the exercise of defining your vision, this is now the top priority. Everything else in your plan hinges on where you want your business to go. By developing your vision statement and clearly communicating it to your team, you begin the process of taking your business forward. There is no magic number of priorities you should identify, but try to avoid identifying too many. In my experience working with clients, if they identify more than three or four priorities they have a tendency to spread themselves too thinly, and their team gets frustrated trying to handle too many strategies. Of course, you may have one glaring priority that needs to be attended to right away, and that may be all you can do in your first six-month plan.

Set Goals and Objectives

Your overall business plan should have two sets of goals and objectives. The first should be your overall business goals and objectives, which include sales, revenue, new customers, profitability, etc. This is the typical set of goals for most businesses. The second set of goals and objectives are the specific goals and objectives for each priority you include in your plan. Set up specific goals, which are keyed into the priorities you have established as the focus for your first six months. These goals and objectives should be what I call "activity-based" or "milestones." They address the specific actions that need to occur in order for you to succeed in carrying out the strategies and tools for each of your designated priorities.

Define Strategies

The next step in making your overall plan is to carry forward the specific strategies you have already identified in going through the Six Key Elements. If you refer to those areas, you will find that for each of the priorities you identified, you also defined the strategies on which you need to focus. In your overall blueprint, or plan document, you must now transfer those strategies to your six-month plan.

A note of caution: if you identified more than two strategies for any one priority, you should determine which two are the most important. By the time your plan is finished, you'll most likely have six to eight strategies on which to focus. If you select more than that, you may run the risk of trying to tackle too much at once.

Let's say you've identified marketing systems as a top priority. As you review that key element you see that you identified four strategies to focus on: existing customers, a new market, a specific product line, and a cold marketing list. Now you ought to pick the two that will have the most impact over the next six months. Those are the two on which your team should concentrate first.

Communicate and Train

The key to the success of any plan is having the buy-in of your team. The next step in developing your overall plan is to communicate exactly what strategies you will focus on and what priorities you have identified. Keep your team involved in the process. It is better to err on the side of too much information rather than the "mushroom management theory," which is to keep them in the dark and feed the ... You know the rest of that idiom ...

Before you introduce your tools, plan exactly what you will need to do to train your team. Think about what needs to be done to get your team members to execute your six to eight strategies effectively, and what training they will need to carry out the tools and tasks.

Determine Tools

As in the previous step, determine the strategies you identified and assign the tools you're going to use to make those strategies work. Using the same process as before, look at the number of tools you selected and then whittle them down to two or three per strategy.

Using the above example, if you decide the two most important strategies are existing customers and the new market, and you identified four tools (such as direct response marketing, email marketing, and advertising and telemarketing campaigns), pick the two or three of these that will have the most immediate impact on your business and concentrate on those for the next six months.

Remember, by creating a plan limited to six months, you can always bring new strategies and tools into play in your next six-month plan.

Create Tasks and Timelines

Once you have determined the specific tools you'll be implementing in your plan, sit down and meet with the team members that will be carrying out the tasks. Go through each tool and lay out the specific tasks that need to be done. When you have discussed each task, the next step is to set up timelines and delegate responsibility for who will do each task and when it is to be finished. In having this discussion with your team, let them have input in creating the timelines; you'll get better buy-in.

Remember, this is a six-month plan and not everything has to be done in the next week. Spread out the tasks and timelines so you facilitate your team's success.

Keep Score and Communicate Results

Key milestones are essential to your plan. Putting in key milestones enables you to track the process on a regular basis—weekly or monthly—and creates the framework for success. Most business plans focus on results and fail. When you focus on the activity needed to achieve the results, you give yourself a much better chance at success. Look at the key milestones at least once a week, and communicate the results of those milestones to your team at least once a month.

MOST BUSINESS PLANS FOCUS ON RESULTS AND FAIL. WHEN YOU FOCUS ON THE ACTIVITY NEEDED TO ACHIEVE THE RESULTS, YOU GIVE YOURSELF A MUCH BETTER CHANCE AT SUCCESS.

Reward Success

The final piece of your overall plan is to determine what represents success. Once you have done that, decide how you will reward yourself and your team for achieving it. Celebrate your successes and celebrate the achievement of your key milestones. As your team buys into the milestones and starts consistently hitting them, you will find your overall plan and its goals and objectives will succeed.

Execute Your Plan

Before all else, commit your plan to paper and communicate it to your team. I remember running my first marathon a few years ago. I signed up on a whim, knowing full well I couldn't run three blocks, let alone twenty-six miles, but shortly after signing up I told everyone I planned to run a marathon. Once I told others what I was going to do, I had no choice; I had to run it. Six months later I completed my first marathon. By committing your plan to paper and announcing it to your team, you take the first step in committing to your plan.

When your plan has been committed to paper, start burning that plan into your brain so you are completely focused on it. What I recommend to my clients is that once the final version of their plan is complete, take it somewhere and get it laminated, carry it around and review it every single day.

If you review your plan every day for twenty-one days, you will have created a habit: the habit of focusing on your plan.

Review your plan constantly with your team and make sure everyone is on board; one bad apple can spoil the contents of a whole barrel. Make sure that not only do you have "the right people on the bus," but also that they are in the right seats. Then manage their execution; manage the milestones. Or, as Jay Abraham says, "Become a milestone maniac." Become totally focused on the milestones—activities—required for success.

When you actively manage your plan, you are also able to "tweak" it as needed. As you go along you will sometimes find something that isn't working the way you had envisioned. When that happens, don't wait for the six-month period to end before identifying the problem and correcting it or changing how things are being done. While you should change some aspects of the plan as needed, I don't recommend changing strategies in midstream. You need to give them time in order to find out whether they are successful or not.

Once you've determined the focus of your plan, the actual creation of the plan and its execution will take your business to new heights. I have seen my clients grow businesses 50, 75, 100 and 200% using this process because it literally breaks down, step by step, what is needed to significantly grow a business. If you embrace the process of creating the plan through the Business Funnel Approach, and then rigorously embrace the execution of the plan, your business will have a chance at great success, perhaps a degree of success you never dreamed you could have!

SUMMARY:
CREATE AND EXECUTE YOUR PLAN

- Your first priority should be to define your vision; everything else follows.

- Take all of your priorities and select the three most important. Then limit yourself to two strategies for each priority.

- Create six-month plans. Don't bunch all the tasks into the early part of the plan; instead, stretch them out.

- Focus on the actions outlined in your plan and measure your results religiously.

Find more tools and resources at www.ultimatebreakthroughplanning.com

8

Final Thoughts

The business planning process has always been a mundane, dry process most business owners go through because they either think they have to have a plan, or their bankers or investors require one. This traditional approach hangs around the business owner's neck like an albatross, and so they look on the exercise as a necessary evil. The document becomes a static piece that should be hung on a wall somewhere versus an active document used to grow the business.

Business planning doesn't have to be an exercise in futility; it should be one of the most exciting times for a business owner. It is a time when you get to imagine all the possibilities of your business and all the great things it can accomplish. I can remember doing business planning

> BUSINESS PLANNING DOESN'T HAVE TO BE AN EXERCISE IN FUTILITY; IT SHOULD BE ONE OF THE MOST EXCITING TIMES FOR A BUSINESS OWNER.

with my partner in our brokerage agency. We would set aside a day or two at the end or the very beginning of the year and map out our game plan. Talking about our hopes and dreams for our company thrilled us. Our discussions would go on into the wee hours and we always came out of those sessions rejuvenated and excited about the potential of our business.

The traditional approach to business planning has been mapped out, discussed, taught, engineered, and diagramed for years; it makes a complex document that rarely takes the business to new heights.

My approach takes a much simpler route. In fact, this approach is simple enough to draw up on a bar napkin while sipping a good twelve-year-old scotch—I speak from experience. The beauty of it lies in its simplicity and the fact that it takes you on a step-by-step journey to creating the business you have dreamed about having. Creating this plan should bring excitement, joy and passion about your business. And if you don't have a passion about your business, then maybe you should find something else to do, because the greatest business plan in the world isn't going to help you.

A Word About Financial Statements

You'll notice that I have said very little in this book about the need to have financial statements as part of your business plan. Of course, I don't mean to imply that you don't need them. Obviously, if you don't have a good handle on your profitability you will certainly have difficulty building a sustainable enterprise. As you set your goals and objectives, you can add financials to that area. The most important set of financials is your income statement and your sales numbers. These are what drive profitability and it is important to include them in your overall goals and objectives. This subject requires its own book so I have not tried to deal with it in this one.

Customize the Plan For Your Business

Whether you own a large company or are a sole proprietorship, this process can be customized for your business. I have worked with everything from one-person sales practices to five-hundred-employee companies, and the same basic approach works with each of them and anything in between. The best way to use this approach and customize it for your business is to look at the Six Key Elements and determine whether or not they apply to your business.

Obviously, if you don't have a team, the Leadership and Team Key Element probably doesn't apply. But at least some aspects of the other five elements apply even to a one-horse operation. As you look at the Six Key Elements you will find that some of them simply are not high priority and can be left out of your plan. Each business is different and each has its unique challenges and issues to deal with, so the process is flexible enough that you can determine what your priorities are. By creating a plan customized for your business and focused on growing your business, you set the parameters of what you need to do.

You have gone to the trouble, expense and time of creating a business, company, enterprise, practice or whatever you call it; you didn't just do it for the hell of it. You did it to succeed! You did it to make money! You did it to enjoy the journey! And yet everything you've been taught about how you take that journey has turned your enterprise into a mundane, boring business plan that only your banker and investors will ever look at. It has done nothing to help you succeed, make money or enjoy the journey.

Nothing gives me greater pleasure than to present a workshop or work with individual clients, taking them through this process, seeing their eyes light up and the passion return about why they started their enterprise in the first place. Your business plan is exactly that: your plan. It should take you on that magical journey of creating something of which you can be proud, something that not only provides a good living for you but also for your employees, and something that gives back to your community and those in need. Your plan can take you as far as your business can go. The simple process I have laid out here can help you on that exciting journey.

In the words of Dr. Seuss:

Congratulations! Today is your day! You're off to great places, you're off and away! You have brains in your head, you have feet in your shoes, you can steer yourself any direction you choose!

Questions and Exercises

Introduction

1. Think about where your business is today. Is it meeting your expectations? If not, what would it take to meet your expectations? More revenue, more markets, more customers, a better team, better service? Write down what your expectations are for your business in the next six months. Don't confuse this with goals as we will get to those later. Create a general statement about what you expect from your business.

2. Now think about execution. What things can you do that can help you focus on the execution of your plan in your business? Here you want to start thinking about how you will focus on your plan. What will it physically look like? (I like to create the plan and then

laminate it so I can have it with me at all times!) What will you do to keep it fresh in your mind? How will you keep it fresh in the minds of your team? Write down the things that you will do.

3. Write down the reasons why you haven't been successful in the past with your planning and what you will do to overcome those reasons this time.

First Key Element: Vision and Branding

1. Find a quiet place to think about your business: why did you create it, what did you want it to do for you?

2. Now visualize what that business could look like if everything was working exactly how you wanted it to work. Write down what's working and be as specific as possible. You want to take this step before you create your vision statement because it can help clarify exactly what your vision of your business is.

3. Next think about your best customers. How do they view your business? What does your business do for them that keeps them coming back? Here begin to define the reasons your best customers do business with you; it will help you begin to create your branding message. You want to duplicate the message that your best customers are sending you. If it's good enough for them it should certainly be good enough for your prospects.

4. In creating your branding message start with a 4x6 index card and create the first part of your message by answering who you are and what you do. Include your team in this exercise and have them write down the answers in two sentences or less. Put everyone's responses on a flip chart or white board and begin whittling it down to one message. Have everyone put that one message on the front of an index card.

5. Now the next piece is to determine what makes your business unique. Have everyone come up with four or five bullet points on "how we do what we do," and again combine those messages on your flip chart or white board and work them down to four or five points on which everyone can agree. Lastly, create a one or two sentence statement about how you are unique. Once you've come up with these put them on the back of the index cards. Now everyone on your team has a branding message that they can begin to learn and use on a regular basis.

Second Key Element: Leadership and Team

1. Have your team complete the exercise from *StrengthsFinder*. Go to strengthsfinder.com or purchase a book for your team members and have them complete the exercise and give you the results. Also complete the exercise yourself.

2. Once you have done that, look at your own strengths
    and compare them to the primary tasks that you do
    on a daily basis. Are you playing to your strengths? Do
    the same for each of your team members.

3. Think about your leadership and especially how you
    communicate to your team. Do they have a clear
    understanding of your expectations and what their
    roles are? Think about how you might communicate
    those more effectively.

4. Write down five things that you could delegate that
    would make you more effective in your role.

Third Key Element: Marketing Systems

1. Write down your primary markets.

2. List all the things that you do to market your business.

3. If you don't have at least four specific things that
    you're doing write down some additional things that
    you could be doing.

4. Now write down any additional markets that could
    be penetrated. What would it take to penetrate those
    markets? What additional research would you need in
    order to go after those markets?

5. In creating your marketing systems funnel, determine
    both primary and secondary markets. Once you
    have determined them (these could also be your

strategies), go through each step of the Business Funnel Approach and develop your marketing funnel.

Fourth Key Element: Sales Process

1. How do your customers purchase your goods or services? Specifically define how they buy.

2. Now look at your sales process and write down some ways that you might sell to your customers better. It could be better presentations, better processes for discovering needs or a way to sell more to your current customers. Here you want to brainstorm about how you can sell better.

3. Next think about why customers don't buy from you. What are the specific reasons they don't buy? And is there a way to incorporate that into your sales process to help you sell better?

4. Once you've answered those questions you can begin to create your sales process funnel. Go through each step of the funnel and determine if your sales process should be a priority. If you've answered the questions above and found gaps in your process you should make this a priority.

Fifth Key Element: Exceptional Service

1. Assemble your team and ask them for examples of when they have received exceptional service. Write down their experiences on a flip chart or white board.

2. Now look at each of those examples and ask, How could we do that in our business? As you go over each example write down how they might apply to your business.

3. Now ask, Where are we lacking in our service? Write down the answers in a separate column on your flip chart or board.

4. Compare great service with what your service is lacking. This will help you determine your priorities and what needs to be developed in your exceptional service funnel.

Sixth Key Element: Strategic Alliances

1. Write down all the strategic alliances that you have now. Don't forget to include your legal, tax and accounting resources as well as marketing alliances and other service alliances such as printing, communication, etc.

2. Now go back to your *StrengthsFinder* that you did in the leadership and team section and determine all the things you are doing that don't fit your strengths. Here

you have two options: delegate to staff or outsource. Write them in two columns, delegation on the left and outsourcing on the right.

3. Now you have determined your priorities for creating your strategic alliances funnel. Look into options for outsourcing, not only in your local market but throughout the world. Outsourcing is becoming very popular; for instance, I use a graphics firm in China and get market research from a company in India. There are many options for outsourcing and creating strategic alliances.

Create and Execute Your Plan

1. Now it's time to create your plan. Go back through the exercises at the end of each chapter. They will help you determine what your priorities should be. List those priorities, and from those, your plan will follow throughout the funnel process.

2. Commit your plan to paper and communicate with your team. You can get planning tools and forms at www.ultimatebreakthroughplanning.com to help you through the process.

3. Once your plan is on paper, look at it every day. The sooner you can get that plan burned into your brain, the sooner you will focus on putting it into action!

Resources and Tools

Vision and Branding

Blanchard, Ken. *Leading at a Higher Level: Blanchard on Leadership and Creating High Performing Organizations.* Upper Saddle River, New Jersey: FT Press, 2006.

Canfield, Jack, Mark Victor Hansen, and Les Hewitt. *The Power of Focus: How to Hit Your Business, Personal and Financial Targets with Absolute Certainty.* Deerfield Beach, Florida: HCI, 2000.

Collins, Jim. *Good to Great: Why Some Companies Make the Leap ... and Others Don't.* New York: HarperCollins, 2001.

Peters, Tom. *Re-Imagine!* New York: DK Adult, 2003.

Ringer, Robert. *Action! Nothing Happens Until Something Moves.* New York: M. Evans and Company, 2004.

Welch, Jack, and Suzy Welch. *Winning.* New York: HarperCollins, 2005.

———. "Winning." *Soundview Executive Book Summaries*, Vol. 28, No. 12.

Leadership and Team

Blanchard, Ken. *Leading at a Higher Level: Blanchard on Leadership and Creating High Performing Organizations.* Upper Saddle River, New Jersey: FT Press, 2006.

Buckingham, Marcus, and Donald Clifton. *Now, Discover Your Strengths.* New York: Free Press, 2001.

Clifton StrengthsFinder. www.strengthsfinder.com.

Collins, Jim. *Good to Great: Why Some Companies Make the Leap … and Others Don't.* New York: HarperCollins, 2001.

Drucker, Peter. *The Effective Executive: The Definitive Guide to Getting the Right Things Done.* New York: Harperbusiness Essentials, 2006.

Drucker, Peter, and Joseph Maciariello. *The Effective Executive in Action: A Journal for Getting the Right Things Done.* New York: HarperCollins, 2006.

Lombardi, Vince. *What It Takes To Be #1:Vince Lombardi on Leadership.* New York: McGraw-Hill, 2001.

Rath, Tom. *StrengthsFinder 2.0.* New York: Gallup Press, 2007.

Welch, Jack, and Suzy Welch. *Winning.* New York: HarperCollins, 2005.

———. "Winning." *Soundview Executive Book Summaries*, Vol. 28, No. 12.

Marketing Systems

Kennedy, Dan. *The Best of Dan Kennedy.* Towsend, Maryland: Glazer Kennedy, 2002.

Kennedy, Dan. *The Ultimate Marketing Plan: Find Your Hook. Communicate Your Message. Make Your Mark.* Cincinnati: Adams Media Corporation, 2006.

Peters, Tom. *Re-Imagine!* New York: DK Adult, 2003.

Sales Process

Duncan, Todd. *High Trust Selling: Make More Money in Less Time with Less Stress.* Nashville: Thomas Nelson, 2007.

Kennedy, Dan. *No B.S. Sales Success: The Ultimate No Holds Barred, Kick Butt, Take No Prisoners & Make Tons of Money Guide.* Irvine, California: Entrepreneur Press, 2004.

Thull, Jeff. *Exceptional Selling: How the Best Connect and Win in High Stakes Sales.* Hoboken, New Jersey: John Wiley & Sons, 2006.

Tracy, Brian. *Goals: How to Get Everything You Want—Faster Than You Ever Thought Possible.* San Francisco: Berrett-Koehler Publishers, 2003.

Exceptional Service

Blanchard, Ken, and Sheldon Bowles. *Raving Fans!: A Revolutionary Approach to Customer Service.* New York: William Morrow, 1993.

Levine, Michael. *Broken Windows, Broken Business: How the Smallest Remedies Reap the Biggest Rewards.* New York: Business Plus, 2006.

Michelli, Joseph. *The Starbucks Experience: 5 Principles for Turning Ordinary Into Extraordinary.* New York: McGraw-Hill, 2006.

Peters, Tom. *Re-Imagine!* New York: DK Adult, 2003.

Strategic Alliances

Collins, Jim. *Good to Great: Why Some Companies Make the Leap ... and Others Don't.* New York: HarperCollins, 2001.

Drucker, Peter, and Joseph Maciariello. *The Effective Executive in Action: A Journal for Getting the Right Things Done.* New York: HarperCollins, 2006.

Please visit Mike Ferrell's website at
www.ultimatebreakthroughplanning.com
for further resources.

Acknowledgements

A conversation with my friend Ian Graham Leask—in the steam room of our sports and health club—ignited my motivation to write this book. As a result Ian became my editor and publisher. Ian, thanks for encouraging me, prodding me and overseeing the completion of this project. I want to thank Ian's whole team at Scarletta Press, and particularly Nancy Tuminelly and her team at Mighty Media—I couldn't have pulled this off without any of you. Also I would be remiss if I didn't thank all those who contributed to the material in the book, especially my clients Steve Grice and Bill Conwell, and former clients Scott Hansen and Angela Boersma and Barney Adams. Thanks also to all my former business partners, especially Bill Dolan and Herb Perry. Over the years I have had the privilege to work with many different businesses and have learned much from each of those experiences, so thanks to all of you who brought me into your businesses to brainstorm about growth. I sincerely appreciate your support. Thanks to my mom, who is my rock, and the real writer in the family. She has always been there with encouraging words and support. Thanks to my dad, who instilled in me the entrepreneurial spirit at a very young age and whose success in business I can only hope to emulate. And to my wife Susan who has stood by my side through the good times and bad—the roller coaster of entrepreneurship—and supported me and encouraged me with loyalty and passion.

Author Bio

MIKE FERRELL, a graduate of the University of St. Thomas in Saint Paul, Minnesota, is president and CEO of The Pinecrest Group. Mike works with companies and sales practices, helping them create focus in their strategic planning, business development and marketing. He has been involved in eight start-up businesses and has worked with numerous companies, big and small, throughout the United States. He conducts motivational seminars and coaches in the areas of leadership, sales development, sales management and marketing systems. Over the past 20 years he has worked with thousands of sales people and many small businesses, helping them create a game plan to achieve success. He lives in the Twin Cities. To learn more about Mike's work, visit WWW.ULTIMATEBREAKTHROUGHPLANNING.COM.